News Literacy

News Literacy

Helping Students and Teachers Decode Fake News

Robert W. Janke and Bruce S. Cooper

ROWMAN & LITTLEFIELD
Lanham • Boulder • New York • London

Published by Rowman & Littlefield
A wholly owned subsidiary of The Rowman & Littlefield Publishing Group, Inc.
4501 Forbes Boulevard, Suite 200, Lanham, Maryland 20706
www.rowman.com

Unit A, Whitacre Mews, 26–34 Stannary Street, London SE11 4AB

British Library Cataloguing in Publication Information Available

Library of Congress Cataloging-in-Publication Data Is Available

ISBN 978-1-4758-3929-6 (cloth: alk. paper)
ISBN 978-1-4758-3930-2 (pbk: alk. paper)
ISBN 978-1-4758-3931-9 (electronic)

♾™ The paper used in this publication meets the minimum requirements of American National Standard for Information Sciences—Permanence of Paper for Printed Library Materials, ANSI/NISO Z39.48–1992.

Printed in the United States of America

Contents

PART IV: HOW FAKE NEWS PERSUADES   **99**

PART V: PREVENTING FAKE NEWS FROM SPREADING   **117**

Preface

Fake and inaccurate news is damaging to our society. Civic decisions and activities based upon fake and inaccurate news—from TV, radio, newspapers, Internet, and magazines—can have negative consequences for all of us.

Preparing students for more effective civic decisions and engagement—through better understanding of what they see, hear, and read—is an important goal of educators. Recent calls have been made for curricular efforts to develop knowledge and skills in critical thinking, media literacy, and data literacy. This knowledge and set of skills are necessary for students to easily identify and distinguish real, precise news, from false and inaccurate information.

In addition, students must also have the disposition to apply this knowledge and set of skills as part of the responsibility as an engaged citizen. These knowledge, skills, and dispositions are a developmental process that should be learned and started early in school and life.

Fake news is created and disseminated in a multitude of ways. A description of each of those ways or techniques is beyond the scope of this or perhaps any book. However, many of the most common techniques are presented as a necessary introduction of how to distinguish real and fake news.

Fake news can create lies with numbers, as well as words. Methods to identify fake numbers and data, as well as fake words and statements, are also described.

The Checklist Manifesto (Gawande, 2009) supports the advantages of checklists to provide a reminder and protection, so we do not forget to examine all information. Ever looked in the pilot's cabin of an airplane before takeoff? Do we feel better knowing the pilots have to follow a checklist to verify the examination of all information?

Checklists may effectively be used with students as young as older elementary students (D'Orio, 2017). Therefore, checklists are included to assist educators and parents in preparing all students, as future informed citizens, to better evaluate the news—and teachers to fight and correct fake news and information.

More than 100 indicators and techniques to "look for" in identifying fake news are included in this book with minimal use of technical language. The result is this book provides a greater number and variety of ways to objectively distinguish real and fake news than the limited range suggested by some media to "just check the sources."

The authors are nonpartisan. Unbiased real-life examples are included to engage and increase the understanding of the student and citizen across a spectrum of real-life issues. To keep the book at a reasonable length, real-world examples are provided for many, but not all, of these indicators and techniques.

PART I of this book provides an introduction and necessary background information about fake news and information. Examples of the problems and potential harm from fake or inaccurate news are presented. Additional background information is included about the "four hurdles" or reasons for the proliferation of fake or inaccurate news. These reasons include:

- Distrust and doubt regarding what is accurate information in the media;
- Limited personal knowledge and skills to objectively evaluate and distinguish between real and fake news;
- Personal biases that may distort evaluation of the news;
- Lack of personal commitment or disposition to apply objective standards in evaluating the news.

PARTS II and III include chapters that present checklists of indicators and issues to evaluate the news. Each of the chapters in these parts is organized in this manner:

(1) Chapter number and title;
(2) Checklists and description of indicators of the news to "look for" that contribute to accuracy of the news;
(3) Checklists and description, with selected examples, of indicators of the news to "look for" that contribute to fake news,
(4) Description of why the issue is important for determining real from fake news and two discussion questions that educators could use to begin engagement of students in distinguishing real and fake news.

PART II examines the sources and the terms used in the news. A variety of terms, labels, and slogans are presented that a student may encounter in everyday living.

PART III describes methods used to collect, analyze, and interpret information in the news. Only basic mathematical skills are needed and technical language is minimized.

PART IV includes techniques used to spread fake news. Some common misconceptions or fake news in educational practice are described.

PART V provides suggestions for protecting us from fake news. Instructional activities including a sample lesson plan, project-based activity, and a basic fake news bingo game are included. The final chapter provides recommendations for individuals, educational policies, and societal policies to minimize the influence of fake news.

This book can be used as a beginning resource guide for educators to prepare middle school through undergraduate students. Classes in these subjects may be most appropriate: civics; journalism; political sciences; social studies; and social science.

A citizen may use the "look for" indicators as practical survival guides to personally, but objectively, evaluate the news and win the war against fake news. A goal of this book is that we all become "news literate" in distinguishing real and fake news.

Acknowledgments

Robert Janke acknowledges Dr. Bruce S. Cooper's exemplary enthusiasm and guidance. Stephen Coyne gave great technical support in the preparation of documents. My wife, Kathy, provided encouragement during the long hours in preparation of this book.

This book is dedicated to my sons Robert, Ryan, Kevin, Daniel; my daughter-in-law, Emily; my granddaughters Anna, Juliet, and Nora. My wish is that your lives are free from error in finding what is precious and true.

Part I

BACKGROUND AND HURDLES FOR EVALUATING THE NEWS

It is only the ignorant who despise education.

—Publilius Syrus

Fake news has long been part of human history. The danger of fake news, however, is more concerning because our current society has more rapid and diverse ways of disseminating fake news than we have ever experienced.

The first chapter identifies some of the concerns of fake news. Examples are provided of how fake news has created significant and potentially lethal consequences.

The second chapter describes major obstacles or hurdles in objectively evaluating the news. These hurdles are within our society and also within each of us.

Chapter 1

Background

Once upon a time, not too long ago, in a place not too far away.

— Janke & Cooper

Our Founding Fathers fought and died to establish a system of government that supports liberty, freedom, and an inalienable right of people to choose leaders for themselves. However, freedom of choice does not mean freedom from consequences of choice. Protecting that freedom is a necessary duty of citizens to be knowledgeable in identifying and using real news—rather than fake news—as a basis for making civic decisions and engagement.

Fake and inaccurate news has a long history, as indicated by a classic Orson Welles radio "news" program in the 1930s about the Martian invasion of Earth. Reports indicated that many believed the invasion was real and started to evacuate. We can now laugh at the gullibility of people then to believe what to us is an obviously fake news story. Are we now any wiser in distinguishing real from fake or inaccurate news in making better civic decisions and engagement envisioned by our Founding Fathers?

Sometimes, we recognize—but are willing to accept—fake images and news. Do we try to present a better image of ourselves with makeup, clothing, and grooming? Do we recognize the hidden language or puffery in real estate ads such as "needs some tender, loving care (TLC)" for a property and know that may falsely describe a property in need of a significant amount of expensive work? Have we seen signs and ads claiming "world famous" for a product?

News that is unrecognized as fake can create a potentially more significant problem for our society. Fake and inaccurate news may be intended to deceive for the purpose of influencing our decisions. Our concern is that we prepare our students to distinguish real and fake news and that accurate real news is used in the civic decisions we make now and in the future.

3

Today, educators and parents are concerned with the amount of news and different types of news sources available to students on a daily basis, such as the following: social media; TV; radio; Internet; blogs; personal contacts; and even newspapers. Our vocabulary continues to increase with new ways to disseminate information such as with "bots" which are artificial sources, posted as fake humans, to boost popularity of Twitter accounts by appearing to increase the number of persons checking the message.

A person can even buy a bot from a "bot dealer" (Mande, 2016). Increasing the concern with the more rapid and advanced ways to disseminate fake news is a "methbot." A "methbot" is an automated net of bots in a web browser that can significantly increase the count of viewers to increase ad prices. The unusual aspect is that none of the count of viewers is an actual person.

Fake news can now be sent from fake people. Isn't even fake news real anymore?

Fake and inaccurate news have these undesirable characteristics:

- *Fake and inaccurate news can be rapidly transmitted.* The various media and Internet communications have increased the speed and opportunities for transmission.
- *Fake and inaccurate news may not have sufficient filters for accuracy.* Some information may be intentionally fake or false. A tweet from Greg Phillips claimed that 3 million non citizens voted in the presidential election. Evidence to verify this claim has not been provided (Phillip & DeBonis, 2017).

The claim from some states of "massive" voter fraud has been extensively examined, and documented cases have indicated between 0.00004 and 0.0009% of voters (Levitt, 2007). Most cases reflect inaccurate and out-of-date voter registration rolls and record-keeping by the election boards. For example, Treasury Secretary Steven Mnuchin and Steven Bannon, chief strategist and senior counselor to President Trump, are both registered to vote in two states (Anderson, 2017; Kaczynsk & Massie, 2017).

- *Fake and inaccurate news is universal.* The Office of the Director of National Intelligence (ODNI, 2017) released a report alleging the Russians were engaged in cyberwarfare using botnets, trolls, and fake news "to undermine public faith in the U.S. democratic process." This allegation was at first disbelieved by many, but is now widely accepted that many countries in the world also engage in these activities.

Multiple reports have chronicled the village Veles in Macedonia where many residents make money by writing fake news "click bait" headlines to attract viewers and gain revenue. A strange situation is created, since "real" money can be made from creating "fake" news.

- *Fake and inaccurate news can also continue to exist when ignoring accurate, contrary information to existing beliefs.* The National Oceanic Atmospheric Administration (NOAA) reported a rise in ocean temperatures with both a new method using buoys and a previous method of casting a device over the side of a ship. Both methods confirmed the rise in ocean temperatures, but these results may be ignored by those who believe global warming is a hoax.
- *Fake news can have potentially deadly consequences for individuals and society.* For example, Edgar Welch fired shots from an assault-type rifle in the Comet Ping Pong pizza restaurant in Washington, D.C. He was searching for a child sex ring operated by Hillary Clinton and her campaign manager, John Podesta. Mr. Welch read that fake news story online.

A frightening example of potential problems of fake or inaccurate current news was attributed to Pakistan Defense Minister Khawaja Muhammad Asif. He responded to a fake news story alleging that an ex-Israeli defense minister, Moshe Ya'alon, stated Israel would destroy Pakistan if Pakistan sent troops to fight Dahesh (Islamic State) in Syria. Mr. Asif tweeted that Pakistan was also a nuclear state. A potential world catastrophe could have resulted from assuming the fake news was real.

When a citizen takes a witness stand in a court hearing, an oath must be affirmed to "Tell the truth, the whole truth, and nothing but the truth." The proliferation of fake and inaccurate news often seems to reflect a cynical "post-truth America" with a new oath to "Tell not the truth, only the hole-in-the truth, and everything but the truth."

We seek truth in our understanding and in the decisions we make. Truth is a reality supported by objectively verifiable facts. We then use these facts as evidence that supports determining proof or probability of something.

In a court of law, determining objectively verifiable facts is necessary. The collection of these facts is considered as evidence for decisions establishing proof or probability of guilt or innocence. If identifying objectively verifiable facts is important in a court of law, then should we also identify objectively verifiable facts as evidence in the civic decisions we make?

To paraphrase, "All evidence is not created equal." Not all available information is equal for providing appropriate evidence. Evidence is defined in this book as using accurate, relevant, and sufficient factual information for making choices.

Accuracy is the degree to which information is gathered and analyzed by appropriate methods to be factually correct. Accuracy requires the application of professionally recognized and appropriate methods to gather and analyze information in the news that are reliable, minimize bias, and act as controls for other explanations.

Relevance is the degree that facts in the news provide evidence supporting a conclusion or interpretation. A deliberate method is needed to determine if the data or statements support a conclusion or interpretation—and reject the plausibility of other explanations such as context. In other words, do we have the correct facts and information for the conclusion or interpretation?

Sufficiency is the degree that the totality of the facts and information supports a conclusion or interpretation and can dismiss other available competing information or evidence. In other words, do we have enough or complete set of facts or information to support the conclusion or interpretation?

Presentation of facts is the purpose of objective real news organizations and media. Truth based upon objectively verifiable facts becomes a causality of fake and inaccurate news.

In contrast, fake news is defined as information intended to deceive. Here is just a brief listing of many descriptive terms used for the variety of ways by which information can deceive: "alternative facts," bogus, "click bait," confabulated, contrived, dishonest, disingenuous, erroneous, exaggerated, fabricated, faked, falsified, fictitious, fraudulent, half-truths, imprecise, inaccurate, incomplete, irrelevant, insufficient, misleading, partisan, "truthful hyperbole," vague—and many other descriptive terms such as "jokes."

Isn't it amazing that we have so many descriptive terms for fake or inaccurate news? Some of the ways described for fake news may be more difficult to identify. For example, misleading news may be the most challenging to detect because of information taken out of context or a mismatch between a headline and the content of the news (Willingham, 2016).

Fake or inaccurate news is nothing new. Manipulating or "spinning" information—or events—to achieve a goal has been widely used throughout history. Remember the story of the Trojan horse that was used to deceive the citizens of the city of Troy? The horse was a fake offering that the citizens of Troy let into the city. The horse was a deception in that soldiers were hidden inside who then destroyed the city from within. Fake news can destroy a society from within by using false information.

Fake news attempts to create a different reality based upon false "facts." Fake and inaccurate news creates doubt in citizens to objectively determine what is real and what is fake. This doubt fosters less trust in information and in each other, so society becomes more susceptible to conspiracy theories and fake news.

The unsettling observation is that objectively verifiable facts are now considered to be a matter of personal opinion; and, as stated in a recent news briefing, "Sometimes we disagree with the facts." Confusion has also been created with the widely quoted concept of "alternative facts."

Facts are not a matter of personal opinion. Facts should be collected and used as evidence in making decisions. A goal of educators is preparing students with the necessary skills to objectively identify and understand facts to use as evidence in making civic decisions.

"Fake news" has currently acquired an additional potentially destructive meaning and use. The term is now also applied as a weapon to attack and reject any information that someone does not like—or that expresses a contrary opinion.

A deputy presidential assistant stated, "I know what fake news is" (Massie, 2017, p. 2). Unfortunately, the term "fake news" was used to discredit any news outlet that provides information that may be critical of the president. The appropriate meaning of the term "fake news" is information that is meant to deceive. Do we now have "fake" fake news rather than "real" fake news?

How can we prepare our students to be effectively engaged in a world where fake and inaccurate news are the following: easily disseminated; unfiltered for accuracy; universal; considered in place of real or accurate news; and with potentially deadly consequences? How do we prepare our students, as future citizens, to distinguish real from fake and inaccurate news? As indicated in the above examples, our very lives may depend on our ability to distinguish real from fake and inaccurate news!

Schools should begin to teach students to be aware, doubting, and investigating what they hear on TV, read in papers and the Internet. Being skeptical, investigative, and doubtful is not simple; but schools and teachers can begin to show students just how misinformation, lies, and half-truths are possible, and occur in local, national, and even international media. Not easy, but important to think about—and think through—what one reads in the papers, hears on TV, and reads in the Internet. Life is not simple.

President John Adams stated, "Liberty cannot be preserved without a general knowledge among the people." Our responsibility as educators and parents is to ensure that our students and children develop the knowledge, skills, and disposition to evaluate the news in making civic decisions.

The president stated that fake news media are an "enemy of the American People" and that some media provide "very fake news" (Erickson, 2017). Supporting this idea of fake news as an enemy, K. T. McFarland, deputy national security advisor, has been widely quoted as saying that cyberattacks disseminating fake news are an act of war.

If dissemination of fake news is an act of war, this book will provide a call to bear arms in the war against fake news. It becomes our patriotic duty to objectively evaluate the news and as Shakespeare stated, "to unmask falsehood and bring truth to light."

—We need to win this war!—

Chapter 2

Hurdles

The human understanding is like a false mirror, which, receiving rays irregularly, distorts and discolors the nature of things.

—Francis Bacon

Be so true to thyself, as thou be not false to others.

—Francis Bacon

Why is there such a proliferation of fake and inaccurate news? Many reasons exist for why fake news continues to exist. Four dominant reasons or hurdles are described for why many of us are susceptible to fake and inaccurate news. The reasons are four hurdles in the race against fake news.

THE FOUR HURDLES IN THE RACE AGAINST FAKE NEWS

Hurdle 1. Finding Accurate Available Evidence

The first obstacle is that appropriate and accurate news to use as evidence in making civic decisions is sometimes difficult to obtain. Contemporary life has increasing speed, types, and amounts of available information on a daily basis.

However, much available information may be fake or inaccurate and not be objectively verifiable. The intent of some information may be to influence rather than to educate.

Recent polls indicate trust in the national news media is at an all-time low. Many of us feel that we are not adequately prepared to evaluate the news, and that we cannot trust any media or even real news organizations.

Why is the trust in a free press and media so low? Just as Elizabeth Barrett Browning stated "How do I love thee? Let me count the ways." In a similar concept: why do citizens not trust available information? Let us count the ways in the following paragraphs:

• First, many contemporary news media appear to have abandoned the role envisioned by the Founding Fathers. A media–industrial complex business "infotainment" model has been developed using a mixture of opinionated views and outrage masquerading as objective "news" that provokes emotional responses confirming the biases of a targeted group of citizens.

Higher advertising rates and profitability can be generated from the cost-effectiveness in focusing upon a target group of customers with particular beliefs. In essence, the media provide an a la carte menu by which citizens can select what media source they want that reinforces their beliefs.

Alternative available information that disconfirms the belief is demonized and becomes the casualty with this business model. Everyone wins except the typical citizen and the accuracy of information.

• Second, a Fairness Doctrine requiring media to give equivalent time in reporting differing views was eliminated in the 1987 by the Federal Communications Commission (FCC). The radio and television airways are a public resource with many more groups wanting to purchase licenses than available airways.

Publicity and control of the airways are both potential powerful influences upon society that can be used for political or even propaganda purposes. The doctrine was intended to provide a balanced presentation of controversial issues so that the public could be better informed.

Elimination of this doctrine contributed to the growth of more focused and "unbalanced" media delivery in cable television, talk radio, and other media. Despite claims of "balanced" reporting, only a single view or belief is often presented without the need to present alternative views or beliefs—or even concern with the accuracy of the information.

Contrary or disconfirming information is either ignored or demonized—or both. Presentation of contradictory information is no longer needed as the target audience is citizens with similar beliefs. In a strange twist, media presenting just a single view that confirms the existing biases of a group of citizens are more trusted by those citizens than media presenting multiple views.

• Third, an increasing and significant portion of ownership of radio, television, and news organizations is concentrated with a few wealthy families or organizations. A media "echo chamber" has developed in which the same view or message can then be coordinated across different media to control both the content and amount of available information—so that an opinion is the only available message.

- Fourth, a growing industry of fake news organizations has been created, almost as a form of domestic terrorism, to confuse and influence citizens' decisions with distribution of unsubstantiated and inaccurate information or rumors presented as "facts." These inaccurate "facts" are sometimes even submitted to the U.S. Supreme Court in the form of Amicus Curiae ("amicus briefs").

Supreme Court justices have admitted using these unverified "facts" from blogs and non-peer-reviewed data included in the Amicus Curiae as a basis for a decision even if these "facts" have not been properly introduced and examined in the lower courts (Liptak, 2014). The late Supreme Court Justice Judge Antonin Scalia offered a dissenting opinion that reflected the process used in some Supreme Court decisions as "accept the studies' findings on faith, without examining their methodology at all" and the result is "untested judicial fact-finding masquerading as statutory interpretation" (Liptak, 2014, p. 5).

The Supreme Court justices may have as much difficulty as the rest of us in distinguishing real and fake news. A frightening thought is that the justices may not have sufficient training to objectively evaluate potential evidence and may use inaccurate or even fake information as evidence in decisions.

The concern is that the lack of training in the methods and techniques for evaluating real and fake news may have an adverse influence upon judicial decisions. The concept of "fail on standing" is a prerequisite for a court hearing to proceed if it can be shown that an aggrieved party is harmed by an act. Can people be harmed if fake news is used as a basis for a judicial decision? Are court decisions based upon the ideology of the justices or upon the truth of the evidence from accurate, relevant, and sufficient information? Can judges judge?

The concept of *stare decisis* indicates generally upholding precedent of a previously decided case. Should decisions be overturned if fake news is used as a basis for a decision? Is there "obstruction of justice" if the judges lack sufficient training of objective methods to evaluate real from fake news?

- Fifth, using a rationale of "freedom of speech," the U.S. Supreme Court *(Citizens United v. Federal Election Commission)* permitted virtually unlimited amounts of money for anonymous political contributions through political action committees (super PACs). Some individuals have voluntarily disclosed contributions in excess of $10 million.

The paradox is that the judges who are described as "strict constitutionalists" used what may be considered a "loose constitutional" argument to give equivalent rights to corporations, groups, and individuals. Corporations are not "strictly" mentioned with equivalent rights in the Constitution.

This decision creates a greater opportunity for the wealthy to make advertisements of their message as the MOST available message to a wider audience than the less wealthy. Does more money create the possibilities for greater influence upon policies and opportunity to control the message with fake and inaccurate news supporting their views? Does money talk? Does more money give one more speech? What do we think?

An individual is alleged to have contributed millions of dollars in political contributions in her lifetime. The potential influence of these contributions upon policy decisions: "I have decided to stop taking offense at the suggestion that we are buying influence. . . . They are right. We do expect something in return" (Danilova, 2017, p. 4). Are ordinary citizens harmed because of a lack of "equal opportunity" to distribute their message as available information for influencing policy? Does lack of money reduce the amount of "free speech"?

• Sixth, free speech does not guarantee accurate speech. Even the U.S. Supreme Court *(Susan B. Anthony List v. Dreihaus,* 2013*)* has offered only minimal protection from inaccurate and even false political ads. The impression is that the court is more concerned with unbridled free speech rather than protections against fake and inaccurate news.

The court's philosophy is that the "people" are the only judges of the truth and have the responsibility for determining the accuracy, relevance, and sufficiency of information. As a consequence, political ads and some media reports may be so purposively false and provide many examples of the phrase: "Politics is where truth goes to die."

• Seventh, a recent argument has emerged that the job of the media is merely to report news events. The responsibility for determining the accuracy and distinguishing between real and fake news is the responsibility of the citizen.

A "balanced" or false equivalence sometimes reports about both sides of an issue and creates an impression of doubt or controversy, regardless of the quality of the information. This false equivalence can confuse and reduce citizens' trust in the media to distinguish accurate information. Admonishment against a false balance has even been mentioned in biblical passages: Proverbs 20:23 "And a false balance is not good."

A prominent cable TV news journalist, serving as a moderator for a presidential debate, stated that his job is not to be a "truth squad." Another journalist has stated that a "truth squad" to identify false and fake news violates "freedom of speech."

These arguments contradict an important assumption by our Founding Fathers of the role of a free press to warn of inaccuracies. If the media are not responsible for warning of inaccuracies and fake news, then who protects us?

- Eighth, a rationale attempting to absolve the media of responsibility to report accurate information is that a citizen could easily find other fact-checking sources. However, citizens may not know how to access the fact-checking sources and how to evaluate the information.

In this dance of blame, who is at fault: media or the citizens? Will people just believe what they want, no matter the accuracy of fact checking and real news? Does this argument sound as though the media are blaming the victim?

- Ninth, even if fact-checking sources were easily available, the typical citizen may distrust all media, including fact-checking sources such as PoltiFact.org and FactCheck.org. In a paradox, a citizen may not trust the facts reported by fact checkers; and, therefore, may not favor a more factually accurate political candidate or issue.

Josh Mandel, a declared candidate for the U.S. Senate from Ohio, vowed in 2012 to keep repeating his erroneous statements and stated: "In the minds of so many Clevelanders we talk to, . . the Plain Dealer's PolitiFact project is completely biased, sensationalized and without credibility" (Gomez, 2016).

Mandel's comments may reflect a disturbing state of politics. Politicians may now be untruthful without any fear of consequence as supporters will believe them over nonpartisan fact-checking media.

Do we no longer care about facts? A comment was made by Scottie Nell Hughes during a conversation with public radio talk host Diane Rhem, "There's no such thing, unfortunately, anymore as facts" (D'Antonio, 2017).

- Tenth, what about social media? Are all tweets created equal? What about blogs? What about on the Internet? Do you believe that nothing can be put on TV or the Internet if it isn't true? The obvious answer to those questions is that no effective filter exists to identify all fake and inaccurate news.

With greater frequency, however, citizens appear to rely upon the Internet and social media for information as that information is readily available. Many of us assume that every posting is truthful and simply forward or pass along information without checking the accuracy, relevance, or sufficiency of the information.

These open posting and sharing of information create a challenge for the citizen to evaluate the quality of potential evidence for making a decision. Trolls and foreign agents can then exploit the limited efforts to verify information in social media and more easily spread misinformation that may be harmful to our country.

- Eleventh, some available information is incomprehensible to the typical citizen. The use of jargon, technical terms, or poorly explained concepts contribute to limited understanding by the citizen attempting to appropriately evaluate the potential evidence. Many of the terms in the news can be deceptive and use euphemisms or emotionally laden language to influence our choices and actions.
- Twelfth, recent developments have documented computer hacking and the ability to change or modify information on the Internet. Many nations are involved in such PSYOPS (Psychological Operations) activities purposively to spread propaganda and false information to create confusion.

Cyber warfare, trolls from foreign nations, and misinformation are becoming a more serious concern with the quality of available information. "Troll farms" have been established to grow and cultivate false information to harm other countries. Inaccurate information then becomes the weapon of choice with the goal to erode trust in our media and governmental institutions.

- Thirteenth, some professional journals and media sources have needed to redact or remove previously published information. Some of that information may even be false or fraudulent. Readers of this corrected information may then have doubts—or lack of trust—in the accuracy of any information when first reported and believe that all such information may be tainted or fake.
- Fourteenth, some individuals and groups have financial reasons to generate increased advertising revenue. Creation of vivid and controversial headlines and stories called "click bait" are used to attract viewers as additional traffic on their website. These sites may then attempt to sell products or services or to obtain Social Security numbers, bank account numbers, and any other personally identifiable information. These sites are "phishing" for information.
- Fifteenth, sometimes even governmental agencies will purposively try to suppress, edit, or disseminate fake or inaccurate news. The purposes may be to cover up actions or persuade citizens to advance an ideology. The name "Watergate" is almost synonymous with these inappropriate actions.

Recent efforts have been made to funnel, through political appointees, all research results from the Environmental Protection Agency (EPA) regarding climate change prior to dissemination to the public (Biesecker & Borenstein, 2017).

What is a citizen to do when presented with these threats and the rapidly changing and greater volumes of available information that we may not trust? Almost as if shopping at a do-it-yourself market of available information or news, citizens have to obtain, understand, and use accurate real news as evidence for decisions.

Educators and parents have responsibility to prepare students to evaluate and distinguish real and fake news in making decisions. Will our students have the knowledge envisioned by John Adams to accurately evaluate potential evidence to preserve our liberties?

Hurdle 2. Gaining Knowledge to Evaluate Evidence

The second obstacle is that educators, parents, and students may have a bounded or limited understanding of methods used by experts to objectively evaluate the appropriateness of facts and information to use as evidence. Lack of preparation and knowledge to evaluate information may result in "low information" voters who make decisions based upon fake news.

Students need to understand how to evaluate and use potential evidence in making civic decisions. Unfortunately, students are not very good at determining the quality and credibility of evidence that is the foundation of real compared to fake news (Crocco, Halvorsen, Jacobsen, & Segall, 2017).

Limited understanding in identifying accurate appropriate evidence for making civic decision can be enslaving to a society and personal freedom. How can our form of government function without the common basis and knowledge among citizens envisioned by the Founding Fathers for understanding and determining appropriate evidence?

Many potential types of evidence may be available. Students will need to evaluate the quality of the following types of evidence (Crocco, et al., 2017):

- Statistical,
- Research results,
- Expert judgment,
- Personal experience,
- Secondhand experience,
- Examples,
- Laws or policies.

This book addresses all of these types of evidence. Checklist "look for" indicators provide assistance evaluating the quality of potential evidence.

Developing proficiency of students in identifying facts and evaluating multiple sources of evidence for making civic choices continues to be important and is even mentioned as a needed skill for the twenty-first century (AAC&U, 2015). The U.S. Department of Education (2012) has also stated the need for educators to improve the preparation of students for more informed civic engagement. Students need to become more literate in ways to evaluate news.

Most citizens have not received formal training to learn ways of objectively evaluating the accuracy, relevance, and sufficiency of information and the news. How can citizens acquire literacy in understanding and applying the necessary skills for making civic decisions?

Possibilities exist for formal training and instruction. Teacher preparation programs need to include training enabling teachers to provide opportunities and instruction that develop student skills in evaluating information. Without such instruction, the students may not acquire sufficient knowledge and skills to evaluate potential evidence.

However, university teacher preparation programs may not provide sufficient training in the methods and procedures used by experts in evaluating information and the news (AAC&U, 2017). If teachers do not have a full understanding of the methods used by experts, then how can educators develop student knowledge and skills?

Some recent efforts have been made acknowledging the need to teach and require that students learn methods to evaluate and distinguish real and fake news. An example is a proposal in California to develop a curriculum teaching students how to differentiate between informing news and misleading news (Stoltzfus, 2017).

Educators face practical and theoretical challenges in preparing students to distinguish real from fake news and also how to collect and use facts as evidence for making decisions. Here is a partial list of only some of the many challenges in developing and implementing any curriculum:

• What instructional materials and resources?
• What number of skills?
• What level of understanding is necessary?
• What instructional methods?
• How to measure student understanding?

Available materials and resources cover a spectrum from simplistic suggestions to "just look and check the sources" to professional standards that provide detailed and complicated mathematical guides for determining the accuracy. Like the story of Goldilocks, the materials and resources used should be easy to use, but also provide sufficient comprehensiveness. An axiom is true: If the resource is too simplistic, the resource will be of little use; if the resource is too complicated, it will be little used.

A deluge of guides intended to assist in identifying fake news has recently been posted online or printed. Additional guides seem to appear almost daily. Unfortunately, they often suffer from any one of these faults: too general; not comprehensive; a limited range of needed skills; and lack sufficient technical information to evaluate data and empirical information. As such, these guides may have limited use. The following two resources, however, may provide a basic introduction to some of the issues in evaluating the news:

- Valenza, J. (2016). Truth, truthiness, triangulation: A news toolkit for post-truth world. *School Library Journal*, November 26, 2016.
- Herold, B. (2016a). "Fake news" bogus tweets raise stakes for media literacy. *Education Week*, vol. 36 (14), December 8, 2016.

The news is not always as simple as checking the sources. Sometimes the information in the news is more complicated, nuanced, or quantitative. Higher levels of critical and analytical thinking skills are often required. Skills in scientific reasoning, research methods, and data analytic skills are also part of the skill subset needed to prepare students to evaluate the news.

We know what we are thinking. How can we possibly teach our students these more technical skills? Our question in response is: *how can we not teach our students these skills?*

Graphs, tables, and results from a "study," or a statistic are important types of information presented to our students in the real world. Do fake data and statistics appear in fake news? What about fake graphs and tables? What about fake "studies" and fake surveys?

A recent study indicated that 90.3% of teachers believe it is important that students are able to evaluate and determine real and fake data. Do we agree with that result? We just made up the idea of a study and the percentage of teachers. See how easy it is to look like real data?

Professional guides and standards can offer specific, comprehensive, and technical methods to evaluate the news. Those guides, however, are not always written in language that is comprehensible to the typical nontechnical student or educator.

Many professional guides from different educational organizations were reviewed. These guides provide more precise definitions of terms, concepts, and methods used to evaluate information. Here is a list of some of those relevant professional guides:

- Joint Committee of the American Educational Research Association, American Psychological Association, and National Council on Measurement in Education. (2014). Standards for educational and psychological testing. American Educational Research Association. Washington, D.C.
- Zedeck, S. editor in chief. (2014). *APA Dictionary of Statistics and Research Methods*. American Psychological Association, Washington, D.C.
- U.S. Department of Education, Institute of Education Sciences (IES), What Works Clearinghouse (2016, September). What works clearinghouse procedures and standards handbook (version 3.0). Retrieved from http://what works.ed.gov.
- Council for Exceptional Children. (2014). Council for exceptional children standards for evidence-based practices in special education. Council for Exceptional Children, Arlington, Virginia.
- Best evidence encyclopedia. (2014). Standards for research-proven programs. Johns Hopkins University.

In addition to expert professional guides and standards, some books have provided a listing of potential common errors in data analysis and research methodology that could generate inaccurate or fake news. For example, a listing of over 300 different types of these errors that can be made in evaluating information for use as evidence is included in a book by Janke and Cooper (2014).

As written, many professional guides may simply be too complicated for use by teachers and students. The challenge is to present this technical specificity and comprehensiveness, using understandable language that encourages teachers and students to connect their understanding to real-life decisions as engaged citizens.

We should not expect teachers and students to acquire the depth of understanding of experts. Students have differing levels of ability and developmental readiness for learning, and one type of instructional method may not be a "one size fits all."

Even though differential instructional strategies may be needed for students, we can have a goal to prepare all students with at least a functional level of understanding of those professional methods and criteria. Failure to achieve that goal for our students may truly place our society "at risk" from the effects of fake news. Widespread ignorance of how to determine real and fake news is the ally of poor or no choice.

Some effort is needed by a citizen to critically evaluate potential evidence rather than just accepting what is presented in available information, but the effort is worth the reward of making better choices. Our liberties and justice are best preserved by the ability of our students, as future citizens, to ask appropriate questions and determine the accuracy, relevance, and sufficiency of the information when making civic decisions.

Recent legislation has reinforced the need for educators to become more knowledgeable and understand information and news that can be used as evidence in making educational decisions. The Every Student Succeed Act (ESSA) is Public Law 114–95 passed in 2015. This law specifies different levels of verifiable evidence needed to qualify for grants. Many of the levels and standards of evidence have been directly adopted from the What Works Clearinghouse standards referenced above.

The importance of the need for evaluating and determining quality evidence even extends beyond education. The Evidence-Based Policy Making Commission Act (Public Law 114–140) was passed in 2016. This law established a fifteen-member commission to examine how information is used in program evaluation and continuous improvement.

The increase in fake news, the increase in public laws for identifying verifiable evidence, and the potential consequences for our society create immediate pressure for all of us to become more knowledgeable in identifying real and fake news. The philosopher Benedict Spinoza wrote, "He who would distinguish the true from the false must have an adequate idea of what is true and false." How do educators and students become knowledgeable in identifying real from fake and inaccurate news to become more informed in civic engagement?

Checking all available information and increasing knowledge and skills in identifying real and fake news is not enough. We all have personal filters or biases that we use to subjectively, rather than objectively, interpret and evaluate the news. The next section describes this hurdle.

Hurdle 3. Avoiding Personal Biases

We all have emotions and feelings about persons and events. Each of us is a collage of differing emotions or "animal spirits" such as fear, anxiety, uncertainty, hate, greed, love, kindness, generosity, and many others. This is part of what makes us human.

Unfortunately, many of us rely upon our subjective emotions and ignore or avoid an objective analysis of the news as potential evidence for our decisions. Have we ever made a decision quickly based upon how we "feel" about someone or some event? Did we make the correct decision? Did we make an incorrect decision that we later regretted?

Why do we make decisions based upon subjective rather than objective analysis? The reasons obviously include lack of accurate available factual news information and also our more limited understanding of methods to objectively evaluate the news. In addition, another reason is that making decisions upon an emotionally subjective basis is faster than upon an objective basis. In essence, we do not have to take time to think about what to do.

Nobel Prize Winner David Kahneman compared these competing methods for making decisions in the book *Thinking Fast and Slow* (2011). Thinking slowly requires more time to objectively analyze and evaluate information. Thinking that is fast often relies upon our own subjective biases and the quick mental shortcuts called "heuristics" that reflect these biases. These biases or heuristics are often simple mental shortcuts we use to reduce the uncertainty, fear, and anxiety when we face the increasing volume and complexity of information.

Sometimes, we first decide the outcome or conclusion and then search for any information or "fact" to support an opinion. This is fast thinking rather than slow thinking.

Each of us has multiple biases or heuristics that reflect our prior experiences and attitudes. These biases can create false reasoning that makes us resistant to objective information, but more willing to accept falsehoods and conspiracy theories. Understanding and controlling our personal heuristics or biases may help us make better civic decisions.

We may believe that we have no biases. Realistically, all of us have biases. Some of these biases may seem to be rather harmless such as preferences for certain types of music, clothing, food, or even a sports team.

However, some of our subjective biases or heuristics can potentially be harmful. Do we make inaccurate judgments about others or actions to take and support? Do we trust fake news because it supports our own biases?

We are all susceptible, in varying degrees, to initially being more receptive to believing even fake news that confirms our current beliefs and ignoring contradictory evidence. In a strange paradox, many of us even have the bias that we deny being biased and are confident in our skills to objectively evaluate the accuracy, relevance, and sufficiency of the news!

As we can observe, preparing our students to distinguish real and fake news requires more than just gaining knowledge and skills to identify accurate sources of information and objectively evaluate the news. Students also need to understand and reflect how their biases may distort how they interpret information in making decisions. Understanding their own biases may assist students to resist the siren calls of fake news.

Can educators assist students to understand and minimize the potential distortion from emotions and biases when evaluating news? We first need to provide instruction to students about the variety of different biases.

Various researchers have identified over forty common heuristics or biases. A best-selling book described how we may all be "nudged" (Thaler & Sunstein, 2009) or "pre-suaded" (Cialdini, 2016) in our choices by our biases and environmental factors. A complete catalogue of these biases is beyond what can be presented in this guidebook, but are in resources such as books by Cialdini (2009); Goldstein, Martin, & Cialdini (2008); Janke & Cooper (2014); Newberg & Waldman (2006); and Shermer (2011).

The following paragraphs present the most representative and frequent types of bias that students may experience in everyday living. Examination of these biases is needed for students to begin an exploration of personal biases in their decisions. Additional biases from the resources above may be presented and explored as needed for students at more advanced developmental levels.

(a) An *availability bias* means we may only examine easily available information such as from television, radio, social media, or our friends when we make decisions. This bias is the reason businesses and politicians spend money to advertise. Making a message easily available is important in the distribution of real or fake news.

Concerns noted in the first hurdle are the unlimited contributions to super PAC organizations and the "echo chamber" of increasingly concentrated ownership of the media. The unlimited money and the control of media outlets create unequal opportunities to control what is available information and contributes to the bias of only examining easily available information.

Do we have an availability bias by selecting a significant other from the pool of all people within the country or only from the available pool with our local community, workplace, places of worship, or our group of friends? Should we try to minimize this bias by seeking additional information that may not be so easily available? Do we have the determination to minimize this bias and seek more than easily available information?

(b) A *confirmation bias* is where we only seek and believe information that confirms our current beliefs and ignore contradictory information. As described in the first hurdle, media have been increasingly adopting a model to modify the delivery of information toward an audience of citizens with similar beliefs. The disturbing issue is that elimination of the Fairness Doctrine means that we will not be exposed to contradictory information. In fact, presenting contradictory factual information may not change beliefs, but may make some of us even more resistant to admit to being wrong.

The media sources that we most "trust" may not be the most accurate for potential evidence. These media sources may just present news that merely confirms our existing beliefs. Why would we not "trust" this source since the news from the source reinforces my belief that I am correct?

Research studies have suggested that we interpret facts according to our biased set of cognitive beliefs. The result is that we twist facts to confirm our moral, personal, or group beliefs (Weir, 2017).

Do we live in a cocoon of only listening to the same media channels or sources? Do we just get the news we want to have rather than the news we need to have? Does getting the news from just sources that confirm our beliefs make us more susceptible to fake news and conspiracy theories?

What would happen if we received news from other sources? Can we minimize this bias by objectively evaluating the news from other sources or do we just continue to have the bias of subjectively accepting news that confirms our existing belief?

(c) A *denial bias* is rejecting contradictory information to our current beliefs. Here are some typical reactions some of us may have when first presented with contradictory information that we do not accept (Janke & Cooper, 2014):

- that is your opinion,
- I do not believe you,
- not all scientists agree,
- that's just a theory,
- can't prove that.

Many additional comments and reactions have been used to express a denial of conclusions or news that contradicts our beliefs. Have we ever denied or rejected an unsatisfactory accusation about one of our friends by saying something such as my friend "could never do anything like that"? What if the accusation is true? Would it then have been more appropriate to examine and objectively evaluate potential evidence before making such a statement?

What reactions do you have when confronted with contradictory information or news? Are you able to objectively examine the news or do you just subjectively and emotionally deny the news?

A denial bias creates a difficulty for us in objectively examining the news. As a consequence, we may be more susceptible to deny real news and accept fake news and conspiracy theories.

A denial bias is often a first line of defense when we face contradictory news. The denial initially protects us from the fear that we are wrong. If we deny, then we can avoid the fear of being judged to be wrong.

A disturbing example of this denial bias is the recent report of alleged Russian hacking of American political documents (ODNI, 2017). The president-elect Donald Trump denied the veracity of those allegations for some time, but then accepted the truth of the allegations and also indicated that other countries in the world engage in these activities. What level of objectively factual news do we need to admit we were wrong?

(d) A *cognitive dissonance* bias means protecting a positive view of ourselves and our beliefs by blaming others or circumstances when faced with contradictory negative news. We create personal distance from the mistake or contradictory news by shifting the cause of negative news to the other person or circumstance.

Do we accept full credit for something good that we accomplished, but blame and fault others or circumstances for any problem? Ever hear students say they earned an A, but that the teacher gave them a C?

Do we look for the worst examples in others, but the best examples in us? Do we demonize or blame other groups as scapegoats? Do we ever blame others for our mistakes? Do we discredit information from other media sources or individuals that may present a negative or contradictory view of our understanding or ideas?

Sometimes, media purposively create a "straw man" of an organization, person, or idea that is to be blamed or viewed as a reason for everything that is wrong. This straw man concept works by protecting a positive image of an individual or organization and providing a ready target to blame for any real or imagined negative result. The use of labels is often used to describe such a "straw man" concept.

(e) A *social bias* is pressure from groups, individuals, or authorities to accept a belief or make a choice. We all live in a society in which many group pressures are present.

Are there rules or expectations for how you should behave or beliefs you should have as part a neighborhood, place of employment, or place of worship? Do we feel pressure and a sense to support a particular belief just to be part of a group? Do we wear our team colors and support our local team?

The dynamic of social bias is we may need to feel as part of a larger social group. Television programs will insert a "laugh track" or recordings of laughter to influence our response to join with others in accepting the humor of the program. Some of us are uncomfortable being alone and may even join gangs, clubs, or other types of groups to provide a sense of identity.

Social bias pressure is often exerted in our neighborhoods. "Gerrymandering" is the name of a technique used to draw and establish congressional district boundaries. The concept can be used to have some districts composed of persons with similar political identification. This similarity may exert pressure to accept the dominant political view in the district and neighborhood. Do we join a political party and identify ourselves as a Democrat, Republican, or one of many other parties because of pressure from our neighborhood?

Does each group or organization create an artificial reality with rituals, rules, and a "true" unified belief system imposed upon the members? This belief system may be so strong to be impervious to logic, facts, and contrary evidence. Reality then becomes irrelevant.

A real danger is when beliefs become actions. Pressure may be exerted within the group or organization to conform to or reject contrary news, and "follow the company or party line." Social bias is a fertile incubator for fake news. Dissenting views and news are denied and fake news accepted as almost a "loyalty pledge." Discussion or debate about the accuracy of the belief system is counterproductive and actually makes the group more convinced of its "true" belief.

We are all potentially influenced by environmental and social factors. How are we able to resist the social bias pressure to accept rules and belief? Are we as individuals able to objectively evaluate the news or do we subjectively and uncritically accept the news and beliefs of a group?

(f) An *overconfidence bias* means we exaggerate our skill, knowledge, or capabilities. Here are some statements we may say to ourselves:

- "I know what I know."
- "I am certain that I know."
- "Of course I can do that."
- "This will be easy."

Here is the challenge: we have all made mistakes. What did we do when we made a mistake? Did we accept that we did not know enough or did not have the skills needed? Did we seek additional knowledge or news? Did we deny the mistake or blame others?

Does overconfidence have harmful effects when we evaluate the news? A classic example of the potential harm is from World War II. The Allies were overconfident that the German army could not mount an offensive during December 1944. Information was ignored about the buildup of German troops. The German army launched the offensive called the Battle of the Bulge in which 20,000 Americans died because of the overconfidence of Allied commanders.

Are we certain that we can recognize fake news? Overconfidence bias may prevent us from objectively and closely examining the news because we are so certain that we cannot be fooled. Many tricks, techniques, and distortions can be constructed to make fake news appear to be real news. Overconfidence bias may contribute to the spread of fake news. We may assume we are so sure of our knowledge that we do not do sufficient objective examination of the news. Can we be diligent and check the news?

(g) A *vividness bias* means that we give greater attention and meaning to an event or term that has greater controversial or dramatic presentation. This bias is often and effectively used to create and disseminate fake news. A commonly used term of "click bait" describes news that employ techniques that take advantage of our vividness bias.

Here are some of the common techniques focusing upon our vividness bias:

- provocative headlines,
- moving scrolls across a screen,
- simultaneous multiple scrolls across a screen with varying size and color,

* colorful multi-sensory graphics,
* emotional terms and language,
* language implying controversy, importance, or urgency,
* rapid and short presentation of topics, materials, or video.

(h) A *certainty bias* means that we are more likely to accept information or conclusions that provide us with perceived certainty rather than information or conclusions that provide a degree of probability. You will often here see comments in the real world such as the following indicating how many of us are uncomfortable with uncertainty: "The stock market hates uncertainty"; "I just can't stand not knowing what happened to someone"; or "I just cannot take the suspense any longer."

Fake news often capitalizes upon this certainty bias by making statements or conclusions that "prove" an explanation for an event or promise a certain result. The need for certainty makes many of us likely to accept simple ideas or suggestions offered with certainty rather than other suggestions offered without a certainty.

Accepting the views and positions of partisan groups reduces uncertainty that might result from examination of contradictory views and positions of other groups. The certainty bias, combined with other biases noted above, increases the chance for conformity that reduces uncertainty, but at the price of increased partisanship and less effective dialogue among all citizens.

(i) An *urgency bias* is pressure to make fast decisions because of limited amount of time. Ever hear the ads promoting a special price for a "limited amount of time"? Do we feel pressure to decide quickly without careful review of the information? The viewers, readers, or listeners may perceive a limited amount of time to concentrate and evaluate the information. The result is often a subjective emotional reaction rather than a slower objective analysis of the information. A decision that is made in haste is a decision that we may regret.

Don't believe that an urgency bias affects our evaluation of the news or information? Professional football often emphasizes "rushing the quarter-back." Statistics are kept for the number of times a defensive player "hurries" a quarterback to make a decision. We even use a term of "pass rusher" to describe important members of a team who can influence the quarterback to make a fast decision without opportunity to objectively evaluate all options.

Just as football teams want to "rush the quarterback," teams or groups of individuals apply the same concept in disseminating fake and inaccurate news. Do fake news teams have "news rushers"? The intent of much fake news is to create a fast "hurried" subjective and emotional response that the listener or viewer will forward without careful and objective examination of the news.

This may be an axiom of fake news: Speed becomes the ally of spreading fake news, but the enemy of objectively distinguishing real from fake news. Speed limits are posted when driving a car with a warning to slow down as the life you save may be your own. We should also have speed limits to slow the transmission and forwarding of information until we have opportunity to evaluate the news. Slow down as you drive the highway of news so you can see the dangerous curves and slippery road conditions of fake news. Drive safely!

Students need to examine cable news, talk radio, and Internet sites to realize the many times we use these biases or heuristics. An activity for discussion becomes whether students can recognize and minimize the influence of these biases in making decisions about what is fake news.

Are we able to gain control of our biases in order to more accurately evaluate the news? If you answer "yes" to any of the following questions, then your biases may control and limit your ability to accurately and objectively evaluate the news:

• Do we only examine easily available information?
• Do we only want information to confirm our beliefs?
• Do we discredit any evidence that may be contradictory to our beliefs?
• Do we only have a positive view of our own beliefs and blame others for mistakes or problems?
• Do we accept the biases or beliefs of others to fit in a group?
• Do we have the bias that we are always correct?
• Do we have a bias in being attracted to provocative headlines and controversy?
• Do we have a bias to only use information or news that claims "proof" of an event or suggestion?
• Do we make decisions quickly without objectively evaluating the news?

Don't believe that we have any of the above biases? Think we are always rational and objective? If so, then we probably have exhibited overconfidence in our knowledge.

The reality is that each of us has exhibited at least one of these or other biases in our decisions and that we do so on a regular basis. Here is a brief fictitious or "fake" conversation. An indication of a potential bias is included in parentheses with the statement.

Mary: I saw that scary (vividness bias) headline scroll on my favorite cable TV station (availability bias and confirmation bias) last night about the terrorist invasion that is being planned for next week.

Joe: I don't believe that story (denial bias) as I know for sure (overconfident bias) that people like you just believe anything (cognitive dissonance bias).

Besides, my favorite cable TV station had a fast video (urgency bias) and all of the people in my neighborhood (availability bias, confirmation bias, and social bias) think that is just crazy and that is proof enough for me (certainty bias).

Does that brief conversation sound as though it really could have happened? Have you heard anything similar to this? Are you frightened at how readily these biases and heuristics can become part of our language and thinking about issues?

Mary and Joe did not take time to ask for any other objective information to determine if the news was real or fake. Do you think that either one of them even cared about the opinions of the other? Why not?

All of us may simply carry these biases that we use as shortcuts to respond to each other. We may not take time to completely and actively listen to each other, but simply try to shout down or discredit the opinions of others.

Our society benefits from a hearty and full discussion of issues in the news. Do we even take time to gather any verifiable facts in the news or do we just use fast and subjective emotional statements in thinking? Do our emotions and biases override our reasoning and make us more susceptible to using fake news?

Politicians and advertisers can sometimes purposely manipulate and arouse our biases so that we ignore and no longer consider disconfirming facts. Perception matters so that what people believe to be facts (whether or not actually facts) directs their thinking or choices. John Adams stated, "Facts are stubborn things; and whatever may be our wishes, . . . they cannot alter the state of facts and evidence."

Have Americans stopped listening to facts with which we do not agree and just look for information that confirms our bias? Are we able to ask questions to understand so that we may make better decisions?

Fake news is more likely to continue and grow when we let our biases and beliefs determine what we use as facts rather than let objective facts determine our beliefs and decisions. The damaging effect of our biases and fake news upon society is making poorer civic decisions by which subjective ideology triumphs over objective evidence.

Hurdle 4. Commitment to Apply Knowledge in Making Decisions

We have seen that the courts, news media, politicians, and even our own biases and limited knowledge of evaluating evidence may all contribute to the spread of fake or false news. Citizens need to be personally vigilant in evaluating all news.

Gaining knowledge and skills in identifying fake and real in available news is necessary, but insufficient to objectively evaluate the news and prevent the spread of fake news. Minimizing our own biases is necessary, but also insufficient.

In addition, we need the disposition and the intellectual and moral courage to objectively evaluate the news, acknowledge when we are wrong, and then change our beliefs when more accurate verifiable facts and evidence become available. This is a fundamental basis of our civic responsibility. Our Founding Fathers had the courage to lay their lives on the line to support a change in forming a system of government that supports the inalienable rights of citizens to choose for themselves. Do we have the courage to follow the facts in making choices?

The Constitution of the United States has acknowledged the need for changes. Don't believe the Constitution changes? These changes are formally called Amendments and indicate a civic willingness to change beliefs about such varied issues as slavery and women's right to vote. We may now think that women always had the right to vote, but that right was only nationally conferred in the early 1900s.

We have also made changes in other beliefs in our society with implications for life and death decisions. For example, using more accurate evidence from DNA testing has exonerated those who have been falsely convicted on the basis of other information.

Do we have "rigiditis" where we are too ideologically rigid to learn from our mistakes? Do we simply vote our biases? Are we ready to change your beliefs when better evidence in the news becomes available? If so, then how will we be able to objectively determine the information or news is better and more accurate?

The authors use the term CIVILYTICS to describe the composite prerequisite critical thinking skills, media literacy, data literacy, and dispositions for becoming an informed citizen in evaluating evidence in civic decisions and determining what is true and false. This book contributes to CIVILYTICS by providing an objective and nonpartisan checklist of questions, methods, and information to "look for" to evaluate evidence that students and citizens can apply in their daily lives.

The ultimate responsibility for effective civic engagement and decision making resides within each of us to apply the knowledge and the disposition to change when presented with more appropriate evidence. If we accept this responsibility as a civic duty of citizens in a global society, then we will have a more perfect union that was the hope of the Founders.

The hope is that students will be prepared with the necessary knowledge, skills, and dispositions to fight against fake news with the same fierce determination of Patrick Henry who stated, "Whatever anguish of spirit it may cost, I am willing to know the whole truth." We have a "call to bear arms" in the fight against fake and inaccurate news.

Part II

SOURCES AND TERMS IN ACCURATE AND FAKE NEWS

False words are not only evil in themselves, but they infect the soul with evil.

—Plato

This part of the book presents a variety of characteristics and issues that need to be examined to distinguish between real and fake news. These characteristics and issues provide "look for" indicators that are minimally essential for distinguishing real and fake news. These "look for" indicators do not provide all of the possible ways to evaluate the news, but do provide indicators that give greater confidence to identify real and fake news.

A wide range of needed characteristics and issues to evaluate the news is presented. The students will need to apply relevant skills including critical thinking, media literacy, and data literacy.

The wide range of issues and varying levels of complexity of the "look for" indicators permit an educator to develop instructional activities consistent with the developmental levels of students. Educators can then prepare lessons from basic to advanced levels.

Real-world examples of fake and inaccurate news are also included to engage students in the importance of the topics. The hope is that students will be engaged and prepared to participate as future citizens to identify and use truthful real news rather than fake news when making decisions.

Chapter 3

Sources

Knowledge is of two kinds. We know a subject ourselves, or we know where we can find information upon it.

—Samuel Johnson

Take nothing on its looks; take everything on evidence. There's no better rule.

—Charles Dickens

The sources of news can significantly affect the potential for fake or inaccurate news. We hope the sources have a credible record of providing accurate, relevant, and sufficient information. In addition, the sources should provide information that is objectively verifiable and easily obtained.

This section provides a checklist of issues to "look for" that might increase the probability that the source of the information or news is credible. Another checklist provides issues to "look for" that might increase the chance that the information from the source is inaccurate or fake.

Checklist "look for" indicators of credible news:

- _____Sponsorship of news and reports are identified to indicate any potential conflict of interest that could influence the information.
- _____Nonpartisan sources are used to minimize potential bias and fake news such as:
  (1) Official government documents with an Internet suffix of .gov,
  (2) Peer-reviewed scholarly journals or publications,

(3) Recognized fact-checking sources used such as: FactCheck.org; Pol tiFact.org; Washingtonpost.com/news/fact check; Snopes.com; ABC News (abcnews.go.com).

• _____Official and/or original documents or physical records are used.

• _____Original complete report, questions, and comments are available for inspection and review to minimize inaccurate or incomplete reporting or quotations that may misrepresent by "cherry picking" or taken comments out of context.

• _____Complete description of the methods used to collect the information is provided.

• _____Multiple nonpartisan sources of information are used to provide cross-validation of any conclusion, recommendation, or results.

• _____Use domain names more likely credible, ending in: .gov; .edu; .com; .net; .org.

• _____Copy photo images and drop in Google Images to verify original image.

• _____Sources have a verified record and examples of providing accurate news.

Checklist "look for" indicators of sources news that may be fake or less credible:

• _____Unofficial and/or secondary documents or physical records are used, and this creates possibilities for inconsistent and inaccurate information used as fake news.

• _____Anonymous source(s) not identified may have more potential for bias because of uncertainty and difficulty verifying the authenticity and accuracy of the news.

Example:

Politicians have often stated that the news media should avoid anonymous sources and cite a name for every source. However, a politician cited an anonymous friend of his, "Jim," who now refuses to go to Paris because of the problems with European immigration policy. No further information was provided about the identity of anonymous "Jim."

• _____Sponsorship of news and reports not identified and/or biased with potential conflict of interest to influence the information and suppress contradictory information or news.

NOTE: The term SPONSORED does not mean the news is accurate. The term only means that an organization may have paid to provide the information, and that organization may have motivation to attract your attention with "click bait" in order to create more traffic to the site.

- _____Unofficial documents or sites claiming to be a government or other relevant group, but without the Internet suffix of .gov.

Example:

Expired websites can be purchased. Cameron Harris purchased the website, ChristianTimesNewspaper.com, for $5 from ExpiredDomains.net. Mr. Harris then used that site to disseminate fake news about voter fraud in Ohio (Shane, 2017).

- _____Journals that are not peer-reviewed by scholars in that particular subject and you can check this by both examining the list of the editorial review members for the journal and the affiliation of the professional organization listed for the journal.
- _____Partisan sources may have a particular bias and may be more likely motivated to use fake and inaccurate news sources or highly selective and incomplete information to advocate for a policy and these types of sources include:
  (1) Political ads as these often have a variety of inaccurate and even fake claims to purposely create an emotional response and influence your decisions so you will need to verify the claims.
  (2) Much commercial for-profit talk radio and cable TV news reports as these media may seek to increase ad revenues by presenting news in a manner that confirms the bias of a targeted group of listeners or viewers.
  (3) Blogs, tweets, and other social media as there is minimal protection that the content is not fake news, so verify the accuracy of the content before forwarding or transmitting to others.
  (4) Reports, communication, or "news" from any groups or sources with a financial, political, or religious agenda as these sources may try to use inaccurate and even fake news to promote the agenda.

Examples of only some of the many advocacy groups or news organizations:

American Association of University Women (AAUW),
American Civil Liberties Union (ACLU),
American Legislative Exchange Council (ALEC),
Association of American Colleges & Universities (AAC&U),
Breitbart News,

CNN,
CNS (Conservative News Network),
Drudge Report,
Family Research Council,
FOX NEWS,
Heritage Foundation,
Hoover Institute,
MSNBC,
National Education Association (NEA),
National Rifle Association (NRA),
U.S. Chamber of Commerce,
WikiLeaks,
labor unions,
businesses and corporations.

Do you trust these sources of news? Which sources more than others? Why? Do you objectively evaluate the news from each source or subjectively accept news from that source because that source, even if fake news, provides news that confirms your beliefs? Do you seek information from multiple sources to cross-check the accuracy?

- _____Fake or fictitious organizations that are used to create a false sense of legitimacy of representativeness,

Example:

The Center for Medical Progress *(an advocacy group)* got tax-exempt status for a fake shell company, Biomax Procurement Services. Representatives from the center claimed to be from Biomax and went to Planned Parenthood to obtain medical tissue for research by Biomax. The federal law does permit voluntary donations of tissue only for the purpose of medical research. Agencies providing the tissue may only accept reimbursement for shipping costs.

The representatives falsely claimed that Planned Parenthood was in the business of selling baby parts, and the representatives were then charged with a crime (Weber, 2016). However, the damage from "fake news" was done. Many persons continue to falsely believe that Planned Parenthood violated a law.

- _____Complete documents, including questions asked or comments made, are not available for inspection and review as comments may be taken out of context.
- _____Secondary, rather than original documents, and references are used, such as a summary of a document or an interpretation of a document.

- _____Reference citations of other materials or information used to support a claim are not provided.
- _____Complete description of the methods used to collect information is not provided.
- _____Only a single source of information is used with no cross-check verification from multiple sources.
- _____Source(s) has no specific and verifiable examples of past accuracy of information.
- _____Avoid using Internet domain names more likely to be fake and ending in: .com; .co; .lo.
- _____Photos or video images may be in shades of color, clarity, or context to create a fake or false positive or negative perception.

Example:

Cameron Harris wrote a fake news story about fraudulent votes being kept in a ballot box in Ohio and included a modified photo that claimed to show the fraudulent ballots (Shane, 2017).

- _____Ghostwriters may be used so that a person or organization writes or prepares a report that another person or organizations receives the credit.

Example:

A common practice in some industries is the drafting of a report or research study and then paying someone else with credibility to claim credit for conducting the study or preparing the report. A classic example was Merck, a pharmaceutical company, paying doctors who did not conduct the research studies to list their names as the researchers or authors supporting the safety of the drug Vioxx. The drug was found to contribute to increased heart attack risks and deaths. Merck then agreed to pay $4.8 billion in a settlement.

Importance of the issue:

The sources of information and news used are important for us to consider in efforts to distinguish real and fake news. The simple and often used phrase of "Trust me" is a decision that you need to carefully consider. Trusting the wrong sources can have consequences for all of us.

Ghostwriters are persons or organizations that do not reveal their identity as they write a story or report for which someone assumes credit. Sometimes, a person is also paid to sign or claim credit for a report written or prepared by someone else. The concern with ghostwriters is the difficulty in verifying the sources and materials used to prepare the report or news.

How many times have we seen the phrase "anonymous sources" or a "source close to the president" used in a news report? How can we verify the source and whether the information from the source is accurate?

Fake organizations also create difficulties in gaining understanding about an issue. Whatever our opinions or beliefs about an issue, we must still be aware that advocacy groups may present false or fake information to support a position or idea.

Each of us has made a mistake by trusting the wrong people and being tricked or deceived. None of us want to have the experience of feeling of being tricked. As you see, some sources have greater chance of giving us fake news.

What protections do we have from sources of news that try to deceive us? The best protection is to use checklist "look for" indicators to guide the examination of the sources of information as the checklists improve your knowledge and skills in objectively distinguishing real and fake news. Checking multiple sources will provide opportunities to either confirm or disconfirm the news and determine the news as real or fake.

The phrase, *caveat emptor,* is often translated to mean "the buyer beware." The responsibility rests upon each of us for not be tricked or deceived if we "buy" or accept with fake or false information.

Discussion questions:

(1) Have students make a list of different sources of news. Ask the students to determine which sources are real and which might be considered as fake.
(2) Ask students to justify why some of the sources might be considered as fake news.

Chapter 4

Terms and Vocabulary

Be not the slave of Words.

—Thomas Carlyle

We know how to speak many falsehoods which resemble real things, but we know, when we will, how to speak true things.

—Hesoid

What are they talking about and what do the words mean? Words and terminology can evoke emotional responses and falsely modify the meaning of the news. Language and the words used can have a powerful effect upon how we think about an issue or person.

Terminology can be used to confuse us in believing fake news. We need to understand and distinguish real and fake application of the terms and words.

The first checklist has "look for" ways to obtain accurate understanding of terminology. The second checklist has "look for" ways by which language and terminology is used to support inaccurate and fake news.

Checklist "look for" indicators of accurate terminology:

* ____Official government, dictionary, or professional association terminology is used for all specific terms to provide a consistent base of understanding.
* ____Reference to the appropriate terminology and *operational definition* is provided for the methods and operations needed to measure and verify the meaning and use.

- ____Official terminology is objectively used in the news without elaboration, modification, or qualification.
- ____Terminology is used consistently in the news information.
- ____Examples reported in the news information match or accurately align with the official meaning of the terms.

Checklist "look for" indicators of terms used that suggest fake news:

- ____Unofficial definitions are used in terminology rather than the existing official definitions and some examples include the terms "small business," "poverty," and "family."

Example:

(1) "Poverty" is defined to provide objective guidelines for eligibility for federal programs. Official poverty guidelines provided by the U.S. Department of Health and Human Services (HHS) for 2017 are included in table 4.1. Other definitions or terms may try to create an inaccurate or fake description of poverty rates.

(2) "Unemployment" is defined by the U.S. Bureau of Labor Statistics (BLS) from a random survey of approximately 60,000 households each month and determines the employment status of each person sixteen years of age or older with these several different operational definitions of employment:

   (a) The U-3 report is often considered the official unemployment report. The total unemployed as a percentage of the civilian workforce (employed and unemployed) is reported. Those persons who have

Table 4.1. U.S. Department of Health and Human Services (HHS) 2017 poverty guidelines

Persons in family	Income (in dollars)
1	12,060
2	16,240
3	20,420
4	24,600
5	28,780
6	32,960
7	37,140
8	41,320

Additional 4,180 for each additional person in family.

not actively searched for employment in the past four weeks are not considered as unemployed.

(b) The U-6 report examines the total of all unemployed plus:

    (1) discouraged persons who have looked for employment within the past twelve months, but not the last four weeks,

    (2) part-time workers who are unable to find full-time employment, as a percentage of the labor force and are considered as unemployed, underemployed, or discouraged,

(c) The labor participation rate is the percentage of the population employed or looking for work, but does not count persons who are retired, enrolled in school, homemakers, or who are identified as disabled and unable to work.

These different definitions of unemployment can present different rates. Fake news will often selectively and inconsistently use these measures to present a story or message about employment and delegitimize all of these indicators as not presenting the real employment/unemployment rate. A fake rate is then presented as showing the real rate that is purposively hidden by a government conspiracy. Please make certain that the news consistently uses these officially calculated rates so that you can objectively evaluate employment/unemployment and reduce your subjectivity.

• ____Reference to sources used for the meaning or measurement of terms is not provided.

Example:

Claims that the murder rate is the highest in forty-five years are made without reference to an official document. The official FBI Uniform Crime Report indicates the murder rate of 4.9/100,000 persons is not the highest in the last forty-five years and is significantly below the highest rate in that time period of 7.9/100,000 persons (Lopez, 2017).

• ____Official terminology is modified or qualified to distort the original meaning.

NOTE: The federal government does not have an official definition of *"middle class," "middle income," "rich," or "upper class."* Please carefully evaluate how news uses these terms as these terms may be used inconsistently by different sources or by fake sources to influence our perceptions.

• ____Vague terminology is used that does not permit identification, measurement, and verification that may exaggerate or distort the degree possessed by an individual or event.

Examples:

(1) "Dynamic scoring" is a term or concept proposed for predicting or accounting for the economic effects from tax reform. No official definition or agreed-upon assumptions and methods exist for predicting the economic effects so that the "dynamic scoring" effects can mean anything assumed by those proposing tax reform. Different persons may make different assumptions. The use of "dynamic scoring" can have significant effects for who receives and how much is received in tax reduction or reform.

What assumptions can you make? How about three magic beans growing into a beanstalk so you can reach a treasure in the sky? Why not dream on a big scale?

(2) A common form of exaggeration is the terms "puffery" or "truthful hyperbole" which mean to exaggerate a description of a characteristic, event, or person. We often see this in advertising such as "world famous" for a rather mediocre restaurant. This claim is not verified, but courts have generally been reluctant to find these types of claims as fraudulent. Puffery may not be a French pastry, but can certainly make a lot of dough. Do politicians or sales persons use such techniques to promise more than will be delivered?

(3) Massive voter fraud has been claimed, but actual documented cases have been indicated between 0.00004 and 0.0009% of voters (Levitt, 2007) and in only thirty-one of approximately 4,800,000 voters in the 2016 election in Michigan (White, 2017). Most of these cases reflect inaccurate and out-of-date voter registration rolls by the election boards or a voter may have voted in person having forgotten that he already voted with an absentee ballot. "Massive" is an erroneous and a fake statement to describe any problem with voting. Is there a reason for claiming "massive" voter fraud?

• ____Terminology is used inconsistently by different individuals or organizations in the news media.

Examples:

"bureaucracy,"
"limited government,"
"low taxes,"
"small business."

-     Inaccurate examples are provided demonstrating the meaning of the terms,
-     Emotionally provocative terms or adjectives are used to modify the meaning of terms (table 4.2),
-     Anecdotes or personal stories are used to demonstrate the meaning of a term or concept, but the anecdote either does not accurately represent the concept or cannot be verified.

Example:

An often described story is of a "Welfare Queen" who received welfare checks from the government because of being identified as poor, but drove a new Cadillac. The identity of the woman or the circumstances has never been verified. The anecdote was simply a fake story that was used to misrepresent welfare recipients as undeserving.

-     Personal or "ad Hominin" attack phrases and terms are used to adversely affect the character and perception of another person or group.

Examples:

Donald Trump called Hillary Clinton "crooked Hillary,"
Hillary Clinton called Trump's supporters "deplorable."

-     Subtle "dog whistle" phrases and terms are used as a code for a characterization of others or policies and avoid making an overt negative statement about others.

Table 4.2. Examples of inflammatory words to create negative or positive emotional reactions

Negative emotion	Positive emotion
elitist	common-sense
excessive	moderate
regulated	freedom
upper class	middle class
immoral	moral
massive	modest
onerous	necessary
outrageous	reasonable
extremist	traditional
reckless	careful

Examples:

"public" to mean for the poor,
"urban youth" to mean children and youth of color,
"inner city" to mean negative view of people of color,
"family values" to mean negative view of nontraditional families and individuals such as gay or lesbian,
"welfare state" to mean negative view of service for the poor.

• ____Euphemisms or deceptively pleasant terms are used to create a false and positive image of a potentially negative event or policy (table 4.3).

Examples:

Newt Gingrich, former speaker of the House, wrote a memo in 1994 titled, "Language: a key mechanism of control." The memo was intended for use by the GOP ACTION COMMITTEE (GOPAC) to provide a positive image about Republicans and to attack, influence, and inflame public opinion against Democrats (Stolberg, 2012).

Table 4.3. Political euphemisms

Euphemism word	Potential negative word
revenue enhancement	taxes
senior citizen	old person
disadvantaged	poor
pro-choice	abortion
right to work	no union protection
school choice	not in school with "those" people

Examples:

• ____Slogans or catch phrases are used without complete description as an attempt to convey meaning rather than a full presentation of content,

Examples:

"mission accomplished,"
"make America great again,"
"tax and spend,"
"morning in America."

• ____Labels are given to create a negative perception of persons, groups, or policies,

Democrats could be described with these terms:

"corrupt,"
"dangerous,"
"decay,"
"destroy,"
"enemy of normal Americans,"
"failure,"
"liberal,"
"lie,"
"out of control,"
"pathetic,"
"radical,"
"shame,"
"sick,"
"they/them,"
"traitor,"
"welfare state."

Republicans could be described with these terms:

"change,"
"children,"
"choice,"
"family,"
"freedom,"
"moral,"
"opportunity,"
"prosperity,"
"provide,"
"reform,"
"we/us/our."

Have we seen many of these words still used in political conversations? Why are they still used? Do these words and the language still influence us? How do these words make you feel? Why are words so powerful in influencing our choices?

NOTE: Newt Gingrich was fined $3 million in 1998 by the House of Representatives for unethical conduct.

• ____Term or phrase is often repeated and without further elaboration with the assumption that repetition makes the term or phrase accepted as accurate and increases the chance the term will be more often used and remembered.

NOTE: Here are technical terms for two techniques that are often used:

Anaphora—when paragraphs begin with the same word.
Epistrophe—where several consecutive sentences end in the same word.

Importance of the issue:

Words and terms can create powerful emotional reactions or even acceptance of fake news as accurate. The childhood saying that—"Sticks and stones can break my bones, but names will never hurt me"—is not accurate.

Words can hurt, but they can also soothe. Words can accurately communicate in objective news, but they can subjectively distort and contribute to fake news. We need carefully to examine the words and terms in the news.

Please just pause for a moment and think about the variety of ways listed in this chapter of how words and terms can be used to influence us. Labels, euphemisms, "dog whistles," emotionally provocative words, vague terminology, and unofficial terminology can all be used to produce negative or positive emotional responses. Have you read or heard any of these words and terms in the news?

We can be manipulated with words and terms. The words and terms listed and described in this chapter can affect our understanding and decision making. "Right to work" is now openly promoted with the ideal of "freedom." Does this freedom mean that a worker has fewer protections than offered from collective or union representation? Words are powerful and can inspire, inflame, or illuminate.

George Orwell's novel *Nineteen Eight-Four* has a recent resurgence in popularity. The novel describes how words can be modified as "newspeak" to create different meanings. That newspeak language then controls and manipulates the fictional totalitarian society of Oceania. The unresolved question is whether the language of fake news will control and contribute to a totalitarian society. Is Big Brother in a conspiracy to control our society?

Are we attracted to provocative or shocking "click bait" headlines in online news? Are we more attentive with any of these words boldly and vividly listed on a TV screen or in online news? Just look at these words:

BREAKING;
DEVELOPING;
JUST IN;
TRENDING;
URGENT.

See how easy it is to get your attention with just using a few words? These words suggest the possibility of some event that may affect us so we then continue to pay attention to the rest of the message.

Here is a suggestion if you are ever in a dangerous situation. Yelling "Fire" will cause other persons to come and see if we have a problem because the problem may affect them. Yelling "Help" may not cause anyone to assist us because the problem may not affect them. Choosing the appropriate words can have life and death consequences.

Do we feel any emotional reaction to the different types of words and terms described in this chapter? Are words like these used to make us feel emotions so that we do not carefully think about a suggestion in the news? Do these words make us want to support or reject an idea without even looking at the idea? Can we think of other words that make us feel any of these emotions: angry, fearful, happy, safe? Are we more likely to be influenced by fear or happiness? Why?

The proliferation of fake news in our society almost seems as though we live in a Garden of Exaggeration where talking snakes tempt us to "eat the apples" of fake news. The forbidden fruit can be attractive, but consuming the fake news can be hazardous to our health.

Slow down and try to think about and evaluate the news that we see, read, or hear. Almost nothing is truly so urgent that we have to immediately respond or forward to someone else. Fake news thrives in an environment of rapid and uncritical evaluation of the news. A motto in responding or transmitting news might be: Slow down, the fake news you share can kill.

Discussion questions:

(1) Have students make a list of terms, labels, or slogans that are often in the news. Ask the students to identify which, if any, are intended by fake news to convey a false impression of another person or group.

(2) Ask students to determine the fairness of using the terms, labels, or slogans to describe others.

Part III

COLLECTING INFORMATION IN REAL AND FAKE NEWS

There is a method in man's wickedness.

—Beaumont & Fletcher

The methods and procedures used to collect the news can affect the potential accuracy, relevance, and sufficiency of the news. A variety of issues need to be considered.

Chapter 5 describes methods by which to collect information from a representative sample or portion of persons or documents. Fake news often has a small sample or a "cherry picked" amount of information that presents a distorted and biased conclusion.

Chapter 6 presents different methods and instruments used to collect information included in the news. Fake news will tend to use inappropriate procedures or only a single method to collect the information. Fake news will use inappropriate question wording in questionnaires and poorly constructed tests to generate results.

Chapter 7 includes examples of how fake news deceives with the use of graphs, tables, and adjusted scores. Distorted and cut off tables and graphs, grouped categories of scores, and adjusting scores all are potential ways to provide inaccurate and even fake news to influence others.

Chapter 8 presents some commonly misused quantitative scores used with fake news. These scores are the "average" and "correlation" that have a history of suggesting fake representation of a typical person or of indicating a fake causal relation. "Percentiles" and "grade equivalent" scores are also presented with caution for use in educational practice.

Chapter 9 addresses the concerns regarding interpreting the quantitative and other information. Lack of clarity of assumptions, measurement errors, counterfactual thinking, and failure to examine alternative explanation contribute to fake news often claiming "proof" or "disproof" rather than interpretations based upon probability.

Chapter 10 examines how fake news makes promises or recommendations without sufficient indication of assumptions and qualifiers to permit verification of feasibility and potential success. Fake news can make promises. Reality may be different.

Chapter 5

Obtaining a Sample of Persons or Documents

By a small sample we may judge of the whole piece.

—Cervantes

That's the news from Lake Wobegon, where all the women are strong, the men are good-looking, and all the children are above average.

—Garrison Keillor

The methods used to collect the information from a sample of persons or documents contribute to the possibility of inaccurate or fake news. The amount of information needs to be as complete as possible to ensure sufficient understanding in distinguishing real and fake news. The number of and representativeness of persons and documents significantly affects the accuracy, relevance, and sufficiency of the information. A small and/or unrepresentative sample of persons or documents is a main technique of fake news.

The first checklist below has "look for" ways to determine that the news has a representative and sufficient sample of persons or documents. Objective suggestions are made of methods to minimize bias and to provide greater assurance that the news is more credible.

The second checklist provides "look for" ways indicating the methods used to obtain a sample of persons or documents may yield biased or insufficient information. Fake and false news often depend upon biased methods and a limited amount of information to support a fake statement or conclusion.

Checklist "look for" indicators of unbiased methods and sufficient amount of information:

- ____If a sample of persons is used, then the sample should be obtained with *each* of these procedural safeguards:
  (1) Individuals are selected in a random method.
  (2) Proportion of individuals in the sample who have a particular characteristic (age, gender, income, education, etc.) should match the proportion in the larger group to which results are generalized.
  (3) Sample is sufficiently large with at least 30 in an experimental study and 1,000 in a national survey.
  (4) Volunteers are not part of the sample.
  (5) Percentage of individuals selected who decline to participate or return documents is reported and should be less than 30%.
- ____Complete and original documents, experimental results, and transcript of commentary or testimony are available for review to verify accuracy and completeness.
- ____Direct quotations from documents should also include additional information to indicate the context and minimize possibility of "cherry picked" or selective comments.
- ____Information collected from secondary sources should be so noted as secondary sources may have inaccuracies or bias in interpretation or selection of the information.

Checklist "look for" indicators of methods and amounts of information might be fake news:

- ____Inappropriate methods of obtaining a sample of persons can produce a bias and fake news that misrepresent generalizing responses to a larger group and includes *any* of these methods:
  (1) Individuals are not randomly selected and this creates potential for fake news if the sample is purposively selected and does not accurately represent the characteristics of a larger group.

Example:

A classic example is Dr. Andrew Wakefield in England. Dr. Wakefield reported results from a nonrandom sample of twelve children that indicated vaccinations caused autism. The sample was not randomly selected, not of sufficient size, and was not representative of the proportion of children in the country with important characteristics. In addition, Dr. Wakefield falsified the data to conform to his own bias.

The result was that Dr. Wakefield lost his license to practice medicine. His fake results have not been supported by any other researchers. Unfortunately, his fake news has been accepted by many parents who now refuse to vaccinate their children.

(2) Proportion of a sample with important characteristics is either not reported or is much different from the proportion of the larger group with those characteristics.

(3) Sample size is so small (less than 30 for experimental research and less than 1,000 for a national survey) and does not provide a sufficient number of persons to generalize the results to the larger group.

Example:

Commentators often try to interview a sample of a few people and then claim that the opinions of those people represent the opinions of the typical American. No mention is usually made about the method of selecting these persons and not all of those persons may have knowledge or be affected by a policy or issue. Are the results from interviewing just a few persons intended to deceive?

(4) Volunteers will respond differently and with different motivations than those who do not volunteer—and this a false or fake result or interpretation.

(5) Response rate is not reported or less than 30% of selected individuals participate and/or return responses, and this creates a biased and misrepresentative sample that contributes to inaccurate and fake news results.

Examples:

(a) Ornstein and Abramowitz (2016) reported that many polls included in the news have response rates as low as 9% or less. This low response rate increases the margin of error and potentially makes the sample unrepresentative of the larger group.

(b) Tani (2017) reported a survey in 2007 that had serious flaws for which the court dismissed the results as not reliable because of a low response rate between 0.5% and 6%. The low response rate, combined with confusing question wording did not permit the respondents to understand and accurately respond to questions and to make accurate conclusions regarding the results.

• _____Media are more likely to report controversial or unusual results from a survey without performing a necessary evaluation of the accuracy or appropriateness of sampling and survey methods. The reported "fake" result then finds a willing messenger for dissemination of the news.

• _____Complete set of documents, results, and comments are either not available or only partially available to inspect and determine whether the information is fake, as fake news more often either does not make available any or complete information to substantiate a statement.

Examples:

(1) Best evidence rule is generally accepted in many legal and other situations where an original and complete document is superior evidence to
an incomplete and/or not original document. The complete and original
document, report, or result permits inspection and verification. Fake
news rarely provides complete and original documents.

(2) A typical congressional practice is to combine several different ideas or
bills into one combined *omnibus* bill. Multiple issues are included so that
objections to one part of the bill can be overcome by support for another
part of the bill. A recent omnibus bill had cuts for Planned Parenthood
with cuts for the military. A decision or vote on such a bill without examining the entire bill can result in an inaccurate decision. It is important to
see the entire document.

Do we see and examine an entire contract or document when we make an
agreement? Why not? Could there be conditions in the "fine print" that we
need to understand?

• _____Direct quote or video presentation without additional information
of the context or preceding events creates a possibility of bias and a fake
impression; and this fake impression is increased with using a very short
rather than a lengthy direct quotation or presentation.

Example:

How many times have we seen words, phrases, or comments taken out of
context or selected to provide a biased conclusion?
A television network did not fully present the comments of the father of
a slain Muslim American soldier criticizing policies. Does the news source
provide biased samples of the news?

• _____Secondary sources are used and that source may have distorted
or falsely interpreted the original sources so that fake news results from
not checking the original sources and simply using someone else's
interpretation.

Importance of issue:
Determining how a sample of persons or of documents and comments is
obtained is important to verify the accuracy, relevance, and sufficiency of the
information from a sample. Generalizing to a larger group of persons or to
the entire document and comments requires following appropriate procedures
and safeguards to minimize the chance for inaccurate and fake news.

Conducting appropriate national surveys is expensive with necessary effort to identify and select persons who are representative of the nation. As we will see in later chapters, greater the size of the sample or number of persons in the sample, greater is the accuracy of the obtained results.

The same concepts operate when obtaining sample of documents. The greater and more complete the documentation, the more confident we are in the accuracy of the information.

Only one situation prohibits seeing an entire document and that is called a *standard protective order* by which evidence in the discovery process in legal proceedings is held as confidential and not made public. The assumption is that making that information available may cause harm. Absent such an order, "sunshine" laws should provide access for citizens to inspect the entire documents and comments of record.

Identifying a representative sample of sufficient size is one challenge. Obtaining accurate responses and information from that sample is described in the next chapter.

Discussion questions:

(1) Have students identify information in the news that was based upon a sample of persons or events. Ask the students to determine if the sample might contribute to fake news by having any inappropriate methods of sampling including: biased sample, nonrandom sample, small sample size, volunteers, and/or low response rate.
(2) Ask students to judge how the inappropriate sampling method contributes to false and fake results.

Chapter 6

Instruments Used to Collect Information

Saying is one thing and doing is another.

—Michel de Montaigne

There is measure in all things.

—Horace

Different methods and the types of information collecting instruments can provide a different understanding of topics. Each type of information collection instrument has strengths and weaknesses in the ability to collect meaningful information for making decisions.

Fake news often relies upon just one poorly constructed instrument that produces biased and incomplete understanding. Understanding the limitations of each type of instrument provides greater protection against the claims of fake news.

The first checklist provides "look for" indicators of appropriate information collection instruments and methods. The second checklist includes "look for" indicators of inappropriate and biased instruments that produce inaccurate, irrelevant, or insufficient information that is often the foundation for fake news.

The results from any information collection instruments or methods such as from a survey or a research study should not simply be accepted as fact. The information needs to be objectively examined for credibility in making our decisions.

Checklist "look for" indicators of unbiased instruments to collect information:

• ____Multiple types of the following information collection instruments provide a more comprehensive and sufficient understanding compared to use of a single type of instrument as each type of instrument may have particular concerns regarding accuracy or relevance and may provide a different understanding:

(1) Tests.
  (a) Potential advantage in that thousands of potential tests are available.
  (b) Potential disadvantages in the cost in materials and personnel time, need for trained administrators of the tests, and tests should have norms or standards for comparison and interpretation of results.

(2) Interviews.
  (a) Potential advantages of interacting with others to obtain detailed information regarding opinions or knowledge.
  (b) Potential disadvantages in the cost in personnel time to conduct interviews, need for trained interviewers, and influence of the interviewer upon answers of the interviewee.

(3) Observation.
  (a) Potential advantages of observing actual behavior and how the context and other factors affect the behavior.
  (b) Potential disadvantages in the cost in personnel time to conduct observations and influence of observer upon behavior of those being observed.

(4) Questionnaires (surveys).
  (a) Potential advantage of low cost in obtaining information from a large number of people.
  (b) Potential disadvantage of low return rate of questionnaires, inappropriate question wording affecting responses, and difficulty verifying identity of person completing the questionnaire.

(5) Physical records or documents.
  (a) Potential advantage is obtaining actual original document or physical evidence.
  (b) Potential disadvantages are uncertainty of conditions or methods by which historical records and documents were prepared and difficulty obtaining complete and original documents.

• ____Complete description is provided for the directions given and procedures for how an experimental research study, survey, or examination of documents was conducted in order to verify or replicate the study and results.

• ____Experimental research studies should use and report *each* of the following procedures:

(1) Use an equivalent control group of individuals to eliminate initial differences between groups and permit more accurate comparison of effects.

(2) Describe what and how the potential cause [independent variable] is manipulated.

(3) Describe what and how the outcome [dependent variable] is measured to determine the effect of the independent variable.

(4) Describe what strategies were used for controlling other threats or explanations for the accuracy of the results.

- ____Surveys should use multiple methods to collect survey responses to confirm results as each of the following methods may obtain different results:

(1) In person,

(2) Landline phones,

(3) Cell phones,

(4) Internet without "opt-in" where persons can choose to volunteer or self-select to participate,

(5) Mail.

- ____Tests are administered and scored by qualified professionals.

- ____Responses by participants are anonymous and kept confidential, so identity of the person is not known and to minimize social bias and pressure to respond with a particular answer.

- ____Information from observations is from using a nonreactive method where the persons do not know they are being observed and the observer does not interact with the persons.

- ____Questions in interviews or questionnaires should use these ways to minimize bias:

(1) Specific terminology for the meaning of words is used and understood by all respondents and includes words such as "many," "few," "sometimes."

(2) Questions include only one topic.

(3) Questions are stated positively rather than negatively.

(4) Questions are stated in noncontroversial or nonthreatening manner using language understood by the person.

(5) Questions are stated to avoid "leading," suggesting one response is better than others.

- ____Full range of options is provided for responses to questions rather than a limited and/or forced-choice option.

- ____Complete list of questions in interviews or questionnaires is provided to allow for examining the questions to determine potential bias or misleading language.

Checklist "look for" indicators of instruments to collect information in fake news:

- _____Only a single type of information collection instrument is used and this increases the chance of inaccurate or fake news as the result may simply reflect the type of instrument used without confirmation with results from other types of instruments:

Example:

An example of why we "look for" consistency in results from different information collection instruments is a situation that we have all experienced in our daily lives. How many times have people said one thing in an (interview) or conversation and then behaved or done something different (observation)? Which information collection is the more important? Why?

Fake news often uses an extreme result from only one type of instrument such as an interview comment or a questionnaire to support an idea or suggestion. Contradictory results from other types of instruments such as physical records may be ignored.

- _____Incomplete or no description is provided for the directions given and procedures for how an experimental research study, survey, or examination of documents were conducted as fake news often does not provide sufficient detail about the directions to permit repeating the procedure and verifying the results.
- _____Experimental research studies contribute to inaccurate or fake results because of any of these procedures:
  (1) Not using an equivalent control comparison group as any obtained results may simply reflect the initial differences between groups rather than the real effects.
  (2) Lack of clarity for what and how a potential cause (independent variable) was manipulated, so difficult to determine that the independent variable was the real cause.
  (3) Lack of clarity for what and how an outcome (dependent variable) was measured and so difficult to determine if outcome changed because of the independent variable.
  (4) No strategies described for how other potential threats or explanations for the results were controlled to minimize false or fake conclusions.
- _____Survey responses collected from using only a single method as each of the following methods have varying degrees of accuracy and bias:
  (1) In-person responses may be fake responses caused by the pressure of social bias to conform.

(2) Landline phones are disproportionate in households with older individuals.

(3) Cell phones are disproportionate with younger individuals.

(4) "Opt-in" phone or Internet responses permit individuals to volunteer to participate or self-select to participate, and this creates a biased sample of persons that misrepresents generalization of results to the larger group.

Examples:

(a) Radio call-in shows and Internet surveys are everyday examples of a biased sample as the opinions expressed only reflect the opinions of those who took the effort and had the patience to call in or "opt-in" rather than the opinions of those who did not do so. Persons who called-in will generally be those with particularly strong opinions that do not represent the general population.

(b) Internet surveys may also have a sampling bias because "bots" and "methbots" can automatically respond multiple times so that a response might not even be from a real person.

(5) Responses by mail may have lower rates of returning responses because of time to complete the survey and also lack of opportunity to seek clarification if a question is not understood,

• ____Tests are not administered and scored by qualified professionals,

• ____Responses that are not anonymous may provide a fake result because the identity of the person is known and there may be social bias and pressure to conform to make a certain answer,

• ____Information from observations may be biased and create a false conclusion if the persons knew they were being observed or the observer interacted with the persons,

• ____Questions in interviews or questionnaire exhibit bias and misinterpretations that lead to inaccurate or fake news in these ways:

(1) Vague language that does not provide specific, objective, and consistent meaning for terms used as different respondents may have different understanding of the meaning of terms and interpretations, so the responses may be inaccurate or fake.

Example:

The terms "pro-life" and "pro-choice" may mean different things to different people as more than half of respondents in a survey defined "pro-choice" as not related to abortion, but rather the opportunity to change your mind about anything (Barbour & Streb, 2011).

(2) Multiple topics in the same question so that it is confusing and unclear to which topic the individual is responding,

Example:

"Would you vote for or against the candidate who wants to reduce spending for both defense and heath care?"

(3) Questions are stated negatively, and this confuses the respondents with regard to what is meant by agreement and disagreement.
(4) Questions are stated in emotional, controversial, or threatening language that creates an emotional response rather than a more thoughtful thinking response.

Example:

"Do you agree with the radical and destructive economic policy of the president?"

(5) Questions are stated that "lead" or suggest one response is better than others and this creates a social bias to agree with the suggestion.
• _____Limited range of options is provided for responses to questions, and this may bias or distort the accuracy of the response and be misinterpreted by fake news to indicate support or lack of support for an issue.

Example:

President George W. Bush said about the Iraqi War "You are either with us or against us." The Law of the Excluded Middle is a technique that forces a choice among limited options. No other alternative was offered such as investigating and using other strategies so the statement created a social bias and a potentially fake result,

• _____Complete list of questions asked in interviews or questionnaires is not provided and this prevents determination of potential bias or misleading language which contribute to inaccurate and fake news.

Importance of issues:
Our decisions are affected by the quality, type, and number of information collection instruments. Seeking confirmation of results or conclusions from multiple and different types of instruments provides more confidence in the results.

Fake news reports are often a mirage that evaporates under the glare of the light of information collected by different instruments. A result or conclusion confirmed from multiple instruments and methods has greater objective credibility than a result or conclusion from only one instrument. Fake news does not survive after cross-examination of information from different instruments and methods.

A common situation that we have often seen is a dramatic court trial on a television program. Attorneys representing the different parties provide information or evidence to support their client. The guilt or innocence of the parties is then deliberated and decided by a jury.

During the trial, multiple types of information are presented. Do some information support one conclusion and other information support a different conclusion? Should all of the information support the same conclusion of guilt or innocence? Why?

The court situation just described is an example of a real-world dilemma. What information is credible? What information is not credible or fake? Forensic errors or mistakes do happen based upon mistaken eyewitness testimony, faulty memory, and inadequate physical lab results or documents.

All information needs to be objectively examined, and we seek confirmation of results from different instruments. Fake news does not require objective examination or confirmation from other instruments. Fake news depends upon subjective or emotional reactions without examination of results from different instruments.

Discussion questions:

(1) Have students identify the type of instruments used to collect information in the news. Ask students to determine if information provided by the instrument is appropriate or if the information is biased and fake.

(2) Ask the students to evaluate which types of instruments are better than others for providing real rather than fake news.

Chapter 7

Types of Information

Statistical figures are . . . historical data. They tell us what happened in a non-repeatable historical case.

—Ludwig Edler von Mises

The medium is the message.

—Marshall McLuhan

The types of information presented in the news can create different perceptions and possibilities for making and distributing inaccurate and fake news. Each of these following types of information pose different challenges determining what is real and what is inaccurate or fake: graphs, tables, quotations, scores, and statistics.

Students and citizens must be fully "armed" and prepared to evaluate quantitative information, as well as qualitative information. Data literacy is a necessary component of being an effectively engaged citizen in our contemporary society.

Fake news is not just in the words and terms used. Fake news can also be reported in numbers and visual information, as well as words. We need to know if the quantitative and visual information is accurate, relevant, and sufficient.

The first checklist has "look for" ways to determine if the graphs and quantitative information are accurately assembled and presented. Using appropriate methods provides greater confidence that information is not biased or fake.

The second checklist provides "look for" ways indicating the information may be fake. Inappropriate methods and/or lack of transparency of methods used increase the chance the information is fake. Fake and false news often uses biased or fake data with limited indications of how to check and verify the data.

Checklist of "look for" indicators of credibility of types of information:

- ____Types of quantitative data collected are clearly presented to permit verification of the information.
- ____Actual rather than estimated or adjusted scores or data are examined.
- ____If estimated or adjusted scores are examined, then official governmental adjustments and procedures should be used such as for "seasonally adjusted" or "net" vs. "gross."
- ____Calculations based upon specific individual scores from each person provide greater precision compared to one composite score representing all persons in a category or group.
- ____Time frame period in obtaining the information is indicated with the beginning and ending dates.
- ____Time frame is sufficiently long to determine effects of policies or programs.
- ____Graphs should present information in the following ways:
  (1) Each axis of the graph is clearly labeled with the information represented.
  (2) Lines of a frequency polygon or height of bars in a histogram must clearly indicate if a particular score was not obtained and how many times a score was obtained.
  (3) Equal distance between data points on an axis.
  (4) Full range of individual scores is suggested without a score category that cuts off or "truncates" extremely high ("and above") or extremely low ("and below") scores, but a clear indication is provided if cut off scores are used.
- ____Tables should present information in the following ways:
  (1) Characteristic and the frequency columns should be labeled.
  (2) All individual scores obtained for the characteristic and the frequency or number of persons having that score should be indicated.
  (3) Potential individual scores that no one received should be indicated as "0" in the frequency column. *NOTE:* If the table has more than six potential scores that no person obtained, then those scores need not be included in the table.
  (4) Full range of individual scores is reported without a score category that cuts off or "truncates" extremely high ("and above") or extremely low ("and below") scores, but a clear indication is provided if cut off scores are used,

(5) If scores are grouped into categories, then a suggested minimum of at least six categories should be used with more categories for a characteristic with an extensive range of scores such as income.

• ____Written and verbal quotations are accurately cited and include supporting citations for verifying the quotations.

• ____References to historical documents and events are accurately cited and include supporting citations for verification.

• ____Dependent variables or outcome measures (scores) should permit quantitative measurement and verification such as the following:

(a) Frequency,

(b) Type,

(c) Duration,

(d) Accuracy,

(e) Percentage,

(f) Dollars,

(g) Length,

(h) Score or standard score.

Checklist of "look for" indicators of inaccurate or fake news:

• ____Types of quantitative data collected are not stated or do not permit verification of the information.

• ____Estimated or adjusted scores are used rather than actual scores or data.

• ____If estimated or adjusted scores or data are used, then the method is either not indicated or an unofficial method is used that may contribute bias because of inappropriate assumptions made in estimation or adjustment.

Examples:

(1) Official methods for adjusting scores or data are important to provide a consistent method of understanding. Sometimes, different official organizations have different ways to make adjustments. The U.S. Bureau of Economic Analysis (BEA) and the Federal Reserve have different methods to make "seasonal adjustments" in reports concerning the Gross National Product (GNP), inflation, and other indicators of economic activity. Factors such as weather, holidays, and sales are considered. Unofficial or unstated methods of adjusting information can lead to incorrect or even fake results and conclusions.

(2) Hillary Clinton stated during the 2016 presidential campaign that almost 14 million jobs were created during the years of the Obama presidency. However, that figure was not adjusted for the 4 million jobs discontinued or lost that resulted in a net gain of about 10 million jobs.

-     ____Calculations are not based upon specific individual scores, but upon a composite score representing all persons in a category or group, and these calculations are less precise and potentially biased based upon the number and size of categories.
-     ____Time frame period in which information was collected is either not indicated or may be biased with different beginning and ending dates as slightly different dates may provide significantly different results and interpretations.

Example:

Sentier Research LLC reported that median (typical) household income declined between the two specific months of April 2009 and August 2011; but a sustained improvement was noted in a longer time frame between January, 2009 and August, 2011. The president was blamed for the decline in the short time frame, but was not given credit for the sustained improvement in the longer time frame (Green & Coder, 2017). Be careful what time frame is used. A slight variation can provide a different result and contribute to inaccurate or fake news.

-     ____Time frame period may be inappropriate as either too short to be sufficient to observe effects of a policy or program or too long so that effects may then be diluted from multiple other influences.

Example:

Presidents often claim that rises in the stock market are because of positive reaction to economic policies of the president. However, presidents may be reluctant to claim responsibility for declines in the stock market. How long does it take to determine the success or failure of proposals or actions? Does the time frame make a difference?

-     ____Graphs inaccurately or misrepresent information in the following ways:
  (1) Each axis is either not labeled or is inaccurately labeled, so there is lack of clarity regarding characteristics represented on each axis.
  (2) Lines of a frequency polygon or bars in a histogram do not touch the baseline of an axis to indicate that a particular score was not obtained.
  (3) Data points on an axis are unequal distance apart and this makes an inconsistent representation of change along the axis.

Example:

An inappropriate graph was presented at a congressional committee hearing on September 27, 2015. That graph, as shown in figure 7.1, did not have a "Y" axis scale for consistently determining the number of abortions or cancer screenings and preventive services performed by Planned Parenthood between 2006 and 2013. The numbers can simply be placed anywhere to create a visual effect (Roth, 2015) and a fake impression.

The visual effect indicates that 327,000 abortions performed in 2013 is more than 935,573 cancer screenings and preventive services performed in the same year. Is 327,000 really more than 935,573? Must be one of those new math programs.

An additional concern is that the graph was prepared by an advocacy group, Americans United for Life. We did have an earlier chapter about carefully examining any information from an advocacy group.

Figure 7.2 presents an accurate version of the same information. The "Y" axis scale permits a uniform basis for consistently determining the number of abortions or cancer screenings and preventive services performed by Planned Parenthood between 2006 and 2013. The information in figure 7.2 indicates that the number of abortions performed by Planned Parenthood between 2006 and 2013 has remained within a narrow range. The accurate version of the information in figure 7.2 provides a different visual impression than the inaccurate version or fake news in figure 7.1.

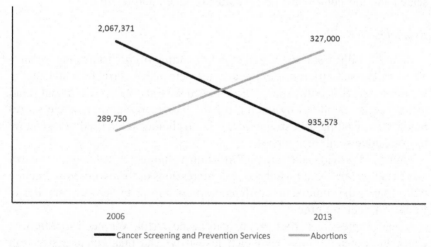

Figure 7.1. Inaccurate Version

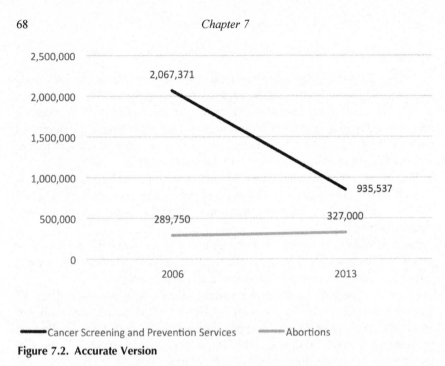

Figure 7.2. Accurate Version

(4) Extremely high ("and above") or extremely low ("and below") scores are cut off or "truncated" so that the full range of obtained scores is not presented and this contributes to inaccurate or fake interpretations,

Example:

Figure 7.3 illustrates the visual effect of cutting off or "truncating" scores. The small actual difference in the average percentage correct for students in the three classes is within the range between 91% and 93%. This actual small difference is magnified by cutting off the bars representing average scores below 90%. Cutting off extreme scores is a technique often used in fake news to exaggerate small differences.

Figure 7.4 provides the same information as figure 7.3, but does not cut off scores below 90%. Contrast the visual impressions of the two figures and you will observe the same actual differences now appear to be much smaller in figure 7.4 than in figure 7.3.

Visual impressions from graphs can be powerful. We need to carefully check the potential ways by which fake news can manipulate and distort information in graphs. Fake news can influence by words, numbers, and visual information.

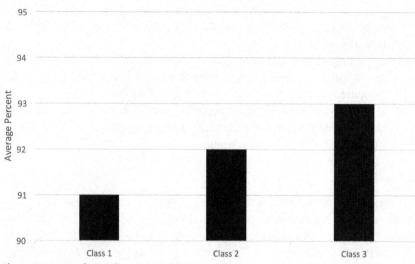

Figure 7.3. Graph Starting at 90 with Truncation

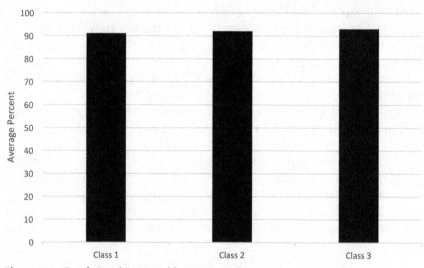

Figure 7.4. Graph Starting at 0 with No Truncation

- _____Tables inaccurately represent or misrepresent information in the following ways:
  (1) Characteristic and the frequency columns are not indicated or inaccurately labeled, so it is difficult to determine how many persons received each score.

(2) Frequency or number of persons having every possible individual score is not reported, so it may distort determining the precise distribution of scores.

(3) Extremely high ("and above") or extremely low ("and below") scores are cut off or "truncated" so that the full range of obtained scores is not presented and contributes to inaccurate or fake interpretations.

(4) If scores are grouped into categories, then fewer than six categories result in less precision with compression of the range of scores and an inaccurate or fake interpretation.

Example:

Proposals are made and discussions held regarding taxation and, especially, any tax savings. Many factors and assumptions are made. Here is a table from a recent proposal that illustrates average assumed tax savings based upon all persons in a category and with categories that have significantly different ranges of potential income. Everyone in a category is grouped together to determine the average regardless of where each person is within the category.

We will explore the topic of "averages" in the next chapter, but for now, please look at the category of income ($143,101 and up). How far is up? Does everyone save $17,000? Is the potential range of income in the category different than the range in other categories?

Could some persons make more than $10 million/year (think professional athletes) and save more than $17,000? The answer is, yes!

Does table 7.1 present information in categories to minimize the appearance of the tax savings of the very wealthy? What do we think?

- ____Written and verbal quotations may be inaccurate or incomplete, "cherry picked," and cited without reference citations to verify accuracy of quotation so that fake news can easily take a comment out of context.
- ____References to historical documents and events are inaccurate and do not provide supporting reference citations for verification.

Table 7.1. Distortion of averages

Income	Estimated average tax savings
$143,101 and up	17,000
$83,300–141,100	2,030
$48,401–83,300	1,000
$24,484–48,400	500
$0–24,800	0

• ____Dependent variables or outcome measures (scores) do not permit quantitative measurement and verification by any of the following:
(a) Frequency,
(b) Type,
(c) Duration,
(d) Accuracy,
(e) Percentage,
(f) Dollars,
(g) Length,
(h) Score or standard score.

Importance of issue:
Fake news is not just in words and statements. Fake news can easily distort graphs, tables, and the type of information.

Visual images in graphs can significantly affect our perception. Cutting off scores or truncating the dimensions is a frequently used method in fake news.

Tables can group scores into categories that reduce the accuracy of determining how many persons received each possible score. The number of categories can change the reported distribution of scores and distort the analysis. Cutting off extremely high or low scores such as "and above" or "and below" is used in tables by fake news just as often in presenting information with graphs.

Fake news will also adjust scores or may use estimated scores rather than actual scores. Inappropriate or nondisclosed methods for adjusting scores can distort obtained information.

Discussion questions:

(1) Have students identify graphs or tables included in the news. Ask students if the graphs or tables show any of the characteristics of fake news.
(2) Ask students to evaluate the intended purpose of the graph or table that might show characteristics of fake news.

Chapter 8

Analyzing Information

When you can measure what you are speaking about, and express it in numbers, you know something about it; but when you cannot measure it, when you cannot express it in numbers, your knowledge is of a meager and unsatisfactory kind.

—Lord Kelvin

Numerical precision is the very soul of science.

—Sir D'Arcy Wentworth Thompson

In addition to the type of information, the methods used for analyzing the information can make us more susceptible to being influenced by fake news. Many "tricks of the trade" have been used to deceive us.

Understanding these tricks helps each of us more effectively to evaluate the news. None of us want to experience the unpleasant feeling that we have been manipulated or tricked.

The common saying that we can make statistics show any results we want is not completely true. Inappropriate methods can be used to provide any desired inaccurate or fake result. Appropriate methods will not always provide the result we want, but will provide the result we need to make better civic choices.

The first checklist has "look for" indicators of appropriate methods for analyzing quantitative data. Detailed mathematics is not included, but the "look for" suggestions provide sufficient understanding of the methods.

The second checklist has "look for" indicators of tricks often used by fake news to analyze information. We need to be prepared to recognize these tricks that are often experienced in our lives.

NOTE: Many of us are anxious about our mathematical skills. Please relax. We are not trying to make each of you a mathematician or to make this a mathematics book.

A goal of this book is to provide a necessary foundation to evaluate quantitative information reported in the news. Increased understanding of quantitative information should assist your efforts in making better decisions and not be influenced by fake news.

A great variety and sophistication of potential mathematical and statistical methods exist for analyzing information. Presentation of that variety and detail is beyond the scope and prerequisite skills assumed for this book.

The mathematical and statistical methods selected in this book represent methods of analysis commonly reported in the news. Fake news can be numbers and statistics just as easily as fake sources and words.

Checklist "look for" indicators of appropriate methods of analysis includes:

- ____Multiple methods are used to analyze the information to permit confirmation of the pattern of results.
- ____Statistical *correlation* only determines direction and strength of a relation between changes in different characteristics and does *not* show cause.

NOTE: Correlation shows direction with (+) indicating a positive relation where scores in different characteristics change in the same direction such as scores increase on one characteristic as scores increase on the other characteristic. A negative direction is indicated by (−) where scores in different characteristics change in opposite directions such as scores increase in one characteristic as scores decrease on the other characteristic.

A correlation shows strength of the relation by how consistent is the amount of change in one characteristic for every uniform change in another characteristic. A perfectly consistent change is either +1.00 for a positive correlation and −1.00 for a negative correlation. No correlation between characteristics is indicated by .00 for a correlation.

- ____Statistical *mean,* called the "average," is reported only as a number that represents the sum of all scores divided by the number of scores and not as a verbal description of a typical person or group,

NOTE: The *mean* can be influenced by a few extremely high or low scores and provides an inaccurate or fake result.

- ____Statistical *median* is the score that half of the frequency of scores or people are above and half are below,

NOTE: The *median* is resistant to influence by a few extremely high or low scores and should be used rather than the mean in that situation to avoid a distorted or fake conclusion,

- ____Calculated measures of variability—such as *range* or *standard deviation*—are provided to indicate the spread of scores with smaller calculated range or standard deviation indicating less variability,

NOTE: Range is a statistical term meaning the size of the difference between the lowest and the highest score in a group. *Standard deviation* is a statistical term indicating how closely the scores differ or deviate from the "average." The same or standard amount of difference from the average is needed for each unit of standard deviations. A score that is two standard deviations from the average is twice as far from the average as a score that is one standard deviation from the average.

- ____Sufficiently large number of scores or persons is used to calculate statistics (correlation, mean, median) with approximately 30 for experimental research studies and 1,000 for national surveys.
- ____Statistical *rate of change* is the percentage of increase between a beginning date and an end date and should indicate the beginning value, the ending value, and the amount of time between beginning and ending values.

NOTE: Lower beginning values increase the possibility of a large rate of change than higher beginning values. Checking the actual difference between beginning and ending values is needed. The rate of change from two to four is 100%, but may still represent low performance. Inaccurate and fake news will use a large rate of change to support a claim even when the actual amount of change is small.

- ____Multiple dependent variables or outcome measures are reported to provide a more comprehensive understanding and to confirm or contradict any other conclusions.
- ____*Criterion-referenced* means the scores or data are based upon comparison to a standard regardless of how other persons performed. The standard needs to be clearly stated and scores should directly indicate how the individual or group compared on the standard using any of the following scores:
  (a) Frequency,
  (b) Type,

(c) Duration,
(d) Accuracy,
(e) Percentage,
(f) Dollars,
(g) Length,
(h) Score or standard score.

• ____*Norm-referenced* means the scores or data are based upon how an individual or group compared to others regardless of how well an individual or group performed. The comparison group is called the *norm* group and should be clearly indicated as an appropriate comparison group. The norm group for school district comparisons in educational practice may be a national, state, or type of school district. The norm group for comparisons for individual students may be age or grade. Any of the following scores or data may be appropriate for norm group comparisons:
(a) *Mean*,
(b) *Median*,
(c) *Percentile*,

NOTE: A *percentile* score indicates the percentage of other persons below a particular score so that a score at the 90th percentile represents performance better than 90% of others. Percentile scores should be used with extreme care as an unequal amount of actual change is between different percentile points as indicated in figure 8.1

A small amount of actual change is exaggerated when individual/group percentile scores are near the middle. Inaccurate and fake news can use this exaggerated percentile change to support a claim even when the actual amount of change is small,

(d) *Standard scores.*

NOTE: A *normal curve* is illustrated in figure 8.1 by which scores on the different scales are arranged with low scores on the left and higher score along the right of each scale. The height of the curve on top indicates the frequency or the number of persons or events with a particular score.

The curve is the highest in the middle of the range of scores and is considered as the "average" or normal score for the group. The height of the curve becomes symmetrically lower from the highest point—meaning that fewer persons or events are much above or below "average." The common implication is that it is "normal" for most persons or events to have about the same score.

NOTE: A *standard score* indicates the number of standard deviations of an individual score from the mean of the group. The vertical lines in figure 8.1

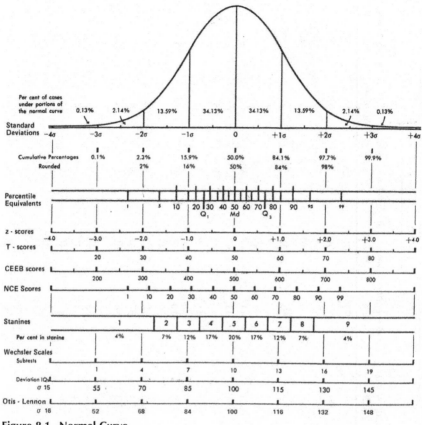

Figure 8.1. Normal Curve

represent the standard deviations from the average. A standard score has a
uniform amount of actual change between each point in a standard score scale
and a uniform meaning across different outcome measures.

The different standard scores commonly used in educational practice have
different "averages" and standard deviations. The *normal curve equivalent
score (NCE)* is a standard score that has an average of 50 and is required for
reporting results for many federal programs. The *deviation IQ score* (Dev.
IQ) is often used to report student ability with a deviation IQ of 100 considered to be at the national average.

These scores can be visually compared in figure 8.1 and also converted to
other scores as indicated in table 8.1.

As an example, a *percentile* of 90 is equivalent to a *deviation IQ score* of
119 and a *normal curve equivalent score* of 77.

Table 8.1. Standard score conversions

Percentile rank	T-score Mean = 50 SD=10	Dev. IQ Mean = 100 SD=15	Stanine	Normal curve equivalents (NCEs)	Percentile rank	T-score Mean = 50 SD=10	Dev. IQ Mean = 100 SD=15	Stanine	Normal curve equivalents (NCEs)
99	73	135	9	99	50	50	100	5	50
98	71	131	9	93	49	50	100	5	50
97	69	128	9	90	48	49	99	5	49
96	68	126	8	87	47	49	99	5	48
95	66	125	8	85	46	49	98	5	48
94	66	123	8	83	45	49	98	5	47
93	65	122	8	81	44	48	98	5	47
92	64	121	8	80	43	48	97	5	46
91	63	120	8	78	42	48	97	5	46
90	63	119	8	77	41	48	97	5	45
89	62	118	7	76	40	47	96	4	45
88	62	118	7	75	39	47	96	4	44
87	61	117	7	74	38	47	95	4	44
86	61	116	7	73	37	47	95	4	43
85	60	116	7	72	36	46	95	4	42
84	60	115	7	71	35	46	94	4	42
83	60	114	7	70	34	46	94	4	41
82	59	114	7	69	33	46	93	4	41
81	59	113	7	68	32	45	93	4	40
80	58	113	7	68	31	45	92	4	40
79	58	112	7	67	30	45	92	4	39
					29	44	92	4	38

78	58	112	6	66	28	44	91	4	38
77	57	111	6	66	27	44	91	4	37
76	57	111	6	65	26	44	90	4	36
75	57	110	6	64	25	43	90	4	36
74	56	110	6	64	24	43	89	4	35
73	56	109	6	63	23	43	89	3	34
72	56	109	6	62	22	42	88	3	34
71	56	108	6	62	21	42	88	3	33
70	55	108	6	61	20	42	87	3	32
69	55	108	6	60	19	41	87	3	32
68	55	107	6	60	18	41	86	3	31
67	54	107	6	59	17	40	86	3	30
66	54	106	6	59	16	40	85	3	29
65	54	106	6	58	15	40	84	3	28
64	54	105	6	58	14	39	84	3	27
63	53	105	6	57	13	39	83	3	26
62	53	105	6	56	12	38	82	3	25
61	53	104	6	56	11	38	82	2	24
60	53	104	5	55	10	37	81	2	23
59	52	103	5	55	9	37	80	2	22
58	52	103	5	54	8	36	79	2	20
57	52	103	5	54	7	35	78	2	19
56	52	102	5	53	6	34	77	2	17
55	51	102	5	53	5	34	75	2	15
54	51	102	5	52	4	32	74	1	13
53	51	101	5	52	3	31	72	1	10
52	51	101	5	51	2	29	69	1	7
51	50	100	5	50	1	27	65	1	1

Here are several types of standard scores widely used. All of these scores only indicate how an individual or group compares to others and do NOT indicate how much an individual knows.

(1) Z-score,
(2) Normal curve equivalent (NCE),
(3) T-score,
(4) Deviation IQ score,
(5) Stanine.

Checklist "look for" indicators of fake news in analysis:

- ____Only a single method of analysis is reported as this reinforces the fake news conclusion by limiting or omitting presentation of any contradictory results.
- ____Statistical correlation is reported as "proof" of causation rather than the direction and degree of strength of relation as the correlation could be "caused" or influenced by other factors.

Examples:

(1) A positive correlation exists between the amount of ice cream sold and the number of people who drown. Does this mean that ice cream causes people to drown? No! More ice cream is sold in the summer months, which is when more people go swimming.
(2) A positive correlation exists between rate of homelessness and crime rate. Does homelessness cause crime or does crime cause homelessness? We cannot determine a potential "cause" as both could be caused by something else such as drug use or unemployment.
(3) A negative correlation exists between the achievement test scores of children receiving tutoring so that the more children in a school receiving tutoring, the lower the test scores in the school. Does tutoring "cause" children to have lower test scores? No! Should tutoring be eliminated in order to "cause" improvement in test scores? No! The correlation may simply be the result that schools with fewer good readers may need to provide more tutoring to assist students.
- ____"Average" is reported as a descriptive term of a typical person or group rather than as the calculated statistical term of the *mean*.

Example:

A classic example is President George W. Bush, during the State of the Union address in January 2008, urging continuation of his tax cuts to avoid a tax increase of $1,800 for the average taxpayer (Blastland & Dilnot, 2009). Although the statistical average was approximately accurate, the fake interpretation was that each typical taxpayer would have that same tax increase.

The average can be affected by a few extreme scores so that average in this example is misleading as 80% of taxpayers would have a tax hike less than the average. When most people hear "average," they interpret to mean typical of everyone. The fake news will support a claim with an average calculated and distorted with a few extremely high or low scores,

- ____Calculated measures of variability such as *range* or *standard deviation* are not provided or are large and suggest inconsistent results or bias from a few extreme scores that may contribute to an inaccurate or fake analysis,
- ____*Median* score is not used rather than the *mean* when a few extreme scores could distort the *mean* score,
- ____Small number of scores (less than 30 for experimental research and 1,000 for a national survey) could affect calculations with a few scores contributing to biased results often used in inaccurate or fake news,
- ____Statistical *rate of change* does not indicate the beginning value, the ending value, and the amount of time between beginning and ending values,
- ____Very low beginning value increases the potential *rate of change* so that little actual change may be exaggerated; and fake news uses rate of change to support a claim even when a little actual change is obtained,
- ____Only a single dependent variable or outcome measure is reported to support a conclusion with no reasons provided for exclusion of reporting other outcome measures that might provide contradictory results or conclusions,
- ____If the performance of an individual is compared to a standard (*criterion-referenced comparison*), then the standard is not clearly stated and/or scores do not directly indicate how the individual compared on the standard using any of the following scores:
  (a) Frequency,
  (b) Type,
  (c) Duration,
  (d) Accuracy,
  (e) Percentage,
  (f) Dollars,
  (g) Length,
  (h) Score or standard score.

NOTE: *Grade equivalent scores* used in educational practice do not mean grade level mastery. A lower grade equivalent score on one measure may actually represent better performance than a higher grade equivalent score on another measure. Inaccurate and fake news in educational practice is often the result of an assumption that grade equivalent scores indicate grade mastery,

- ____If the performance of an individual or group is compared to a group called the *norm* group (*norm-referenced comparison*), then the norm group is not stated and/or is an inappropriate norm group for comparison.
- ____*Norm-referenced* analysis does not use any of the following statistical *standard scores* and/or may inappropriately use the mean, median, and percentile scores without regard to the cautions mentioned in the previous section.
  - (a) *Mean,*
  - (b) *Median,*
  - (c) *Standard scores.*
    - (1) Z-score,
    - (2) Normal curve equivalent (NCE),
    - (3) T-score,
    - (4) Deviation IQ score,
    - (5) Stanine.

NOTE: percentiles exaggerate small changes in student performance by not having a consistent change in student performance to go from one value to another on the percentile scale, as indicated in both figure 8.1 and table 8.1, and should only be used with caution because of the ease of fake news to exaggerate small actual changes,

Importance of issue:

The method of analysis provides a window into examining the extent and type of results in the news. Each method permits a different perspective for understanding. Fake news provides a distorted analysis in which either only a single method is used or the methods are inappropriately used.

We need to become aware that fake news can also include fake numbers and methods to analyze numbers. Fake news influences us with numbers because we may have more limited understanding of how the numbers were collected and analyzed.

Even though we do not have detailed knowledge of all the mathematical processes, we still need to determine objectively real from fake methods of analysis. Developing data literacy is part of the knowledge required to be an informed citizen.

Discussion questions:

(1) Have students identify a news item that includes different types of numerical information. Ask the students to identify the method of analysis used in the news and if the method was appropriate.

NOTE: This may be a challenge for some students so the educator will need to make certain the students are familiar with concepts that are most frequently misused in fake news that include: average; correlation; and percentile.

(2) Ask students to evaluate why correlation does not indicate cause.

Chapter 9

Interpreting Information

It is more of a job to interpret the interpretations than to interpret the things.

—Michel de Montaigne

The public . . . demands certainties. . . but there are no certainties.

—Henry Mencken

How certain are we of the correct interpretation of the news? Fake and inaccurate news often provide interpretations that assert "proof" or "disproof" of a cause or result. These interpretations fail to acknowledge the uncertainty or probability of events and other threats or potential explanations that contribute to false conclusions.

We live in a world where we want certainty. Do we become upset when the weather forecaster cannot tell us, with certainty, if it will rain tomorrow? How do we plan for tomorrow if we cannot be certain?

Checklist "look for" indicators of appropriate methods of interpretation:

- ____Scores should indicate a measurement error (*standard error of measurement*) or how much a score could vary if measured again or was rated by others with a smaller measurement error suggesting more confidence that the score is accurate.
- ____Predicted or projected scores and outcomes should clearly indicate the method of estimation and the assumptions made.
- ____Predicted scores should include a measurement error in prediction (*standard error of estimate*) or how much the predicted score could vary

with a smaller error suggesting more confidence that the predicted score is accurate.

- ____Interpretations are made indicating a level of probability or certainty rather than absolute "proof" or "disproof" with most commonly used statistics requiring at least 90% (.90 level of certainty) so that the probability of chance or another explanation is less than 10% (.10 for statistical significance).

- ____Current information is analyzed and interpreted rather than counterfactual or hypothetical "would have happened if."

- ____Past events and documents are accurately and completely cited if used to interpret current events.

- ____Accurate information is provided for why other potential threats or alternative explanations to the accuracy of the information are irrelevant.

- ____Accurate information is provided for why results are relevant and can be generalized to a larger group, other situations, or other measures.

- ____Group statistics are not used to make a conclusion about each individual in the group.

- ____Statistics from one or a few individuals in a group are not used to make or deny a conclusion about the entire group with any sufficient level of certainty.

- ____Accurate information is provided for irrelevance or probability of other potential adverse results or "collateral damage."

- ____Positive evidence is required so that burden for supporting a causal statement is on the person making a positive claim rather than the burden of proof to negate a claim of causation.

- ____Multiple potential causes, rather than a single cause, for an outcome are noted with varying probabilities for each.

- ____Interprets nonstatistical claims of "causation" by checking a timeline to determine a cause that comes BEFORE an outcome.

- ____Interprets potential nonstatistical "causation" for an outcome or statement consistent with the *Federal Rules of Evidence* where "probable cause" is when a sufficient probability of a cause exists based upon information from a reliable and trustworthy source.

- ____Interprets information regarding accuracy of potential nonstatistical claims of "causation" according to the following levels in the *Federal Rules of Evidence*:

  (1) "Preponderance of evidence" where a statement is more likely true than false,

  (2) "Clear and convincing evidence" where a statement is highly and substantially more probably true than false,

  (3) "Beyond a reasonable doubt" where a statement has no other logically plausible reason to not be true.

Checklist "look for" indicators of fake news in interpretation:

- ____Only a single dependent variable or outcome measure is reported to support a conclusion with no reasons provided for exclusion of also reporting other outcome measures that might provide contradictory results or conclusions.
- ____Scores do not indicate a measurement error and/or the error is large and contributes to difficulty determining a reliable or consistent interpretation of achievement or performance.
- ____Predicted or projected scores and outcomes do not indicate the methods and assumptions and/or the methods and assumptions may not be realistic.

Examples:

(1) Predicting the risk or probability of "recidivism"—or repeating a crime—is now being considered as a factor to set jail sentences for those convicted of a crime. However, the statistical methods used relied upon biased and faulty assumptions since race (black and Latino) contributes to increased probability of arrest and conviction. The consequence is that black and Latino defendants will be rated as riskier than white defendants and more likely to be given a longer jail sentence.

The researchers who developed this risk-assessment model have not released computational details to allow other researchers to determine the accuracy of the predictions (Eckhouse, 2017). Who says that statistics and methods of analysis are not important? These predictions or estimates are used to make decisions about liberty and how long a person remains in jail. It is important to determine the accuracy of any method of prediction.

(2) The lack of consistent assumptions supporting the notions of "dynamic scoring" for tax cuts increasing economic growth has already been presented. The state of Kansas has seen increased budget deficits from such tax cuts and is now having to consider raising taxes because the predictions for income and revenue increase have not been obtained.

Despite the lack of positive economic growth, Ohio and other states continue to follow this concept. The state of Ohio cut the state income tax rate during the past few years. The evidence, however, indicates that per capita personal income of Ohioans is unchanged at approximately 90% of the U.S. average, as it was before the earlier tax cuts (*The Plain Dealer*, 2017).

- ____Predicted scores do not include and/or have a large error of estimate for the predicted score.

- ____Interpretations are made indicating a "proof" or "disproof" as a certainty rather than as a level of probability.

Example:

An example is the statement about whether Saddam Hussain had weapons of mass destruction in Iraq. George Tenet, CIA director, was certain the information "proved" the weapons were in Iraq and stated, "Don't worry, it's a slam dunk" (Leibovich, 2004). No weapons of mass destruction were found, and thousands of military were killed or wounded and billions of dollars were spent on a war.

- ____Results from statistical analysis indicate a level of certainty less than 90% (.90) so that the level of probability due to chance or another cause is greater than 10% (.10).
- ____Current results are either ignored or interpreted with a counterfactual or hypothetical approach that estimates "would have happened if."

Examples:

(1) How many times have we heard our friends, relatives, and even call-in radio programs claim that a result would or would not have happened "if" something else would have been done? This is often combined with the statement from our friends of "I just knew that was going to happen!" or "I told you so."
(2) A concept of the "Butterfly Effect" is used to state that "if only" something had not happened in the past, then our present would be different. For example: "if only" something did not happen to the butterfly, then the bird would have eaten the butterfly and not have starved, then the cat would have eaten the bird and not have starved, then continuing up the food chain. Here is another example that we might see in sports: "if only" the team would have called a different play, then they would have won.

The "Butterfly Effect" is sometimes also called the "future of the past" where we state what our current situation would be "if only" something else had not happened. The difficulty with this concept is that many other potential events "could have happened" that would have changed the current situation.

- ____Past events and documents are inaccurately cited or reconstructed and used to interpret current events.
- ____Inaccurate or no information is provided for why other potential threats or alternative explanations to the accuracy of the information are irrelevant.

- ____Inaccurate or no information is provided for relevance to a larger group, other situations, or other measures.
- ____Inaccurate or no information is provided for irrelevance or probability of other potential adverse results or "collateral damage."

Example:

A recently signed executive order changed the metric to calculate potential damage of carbon emissions upon climate change. Is there any potential collateral damage from change of consideration of carbon emissions upon the climate?

- ____Group statistics are used to make a false conclusion about every individual in the group (ecological fallacy).
- ____Statistics from one or a few events or individuals are used as "proof" or "disproof" to make a conclusion about all events or individuals.

Examples:

Here are two statements that we can hear illustrating the misinterpretation from a just single person or event:

(1) One cold day of weather will make some say: "Guess that proves there is no such thing as global warming."
(2) One scientist might dispute or disagree with the consensus of over 97% other scientists and we might conclude: "Not all scientists agree so it must not be true."

- ____ Negative evidence where the burden for supporting the causation or claim is upon skeptics to disprove, so that if proof cannot explain or disprove, then the claim must be true.

Examples:

This interpretation error is common in fake news and conspiracy theories. Here is a typical comment: *"You can't prove it didn't happen."*

We can add to that statement almost any fake news assertion or any conspiracy theory that anyone wants to develop. Let's try a few and see how easy it is to have fake news so that the fake news story becomes difficult to debunk.

(1) "You can't prove it didn't happen"—that there was massive voter fraud.
(2) "You can't prove it didn't happen"—of a conspiracy to fix the election.

(3) "You can't prove it didn't happen"—[*FILL IN THIS BLANK WITH ANY OTHER CLAIM OR CONSPIRACY THEORY FROM FAKE NEWS—Go ahead as this is what fake news does.*]

The danger with this thinking is the difficulty of disproving the story so we then think the story is not "disproven" so it must be correct. Fake news extensively uses this technique as a basis for conspiracy theories.

• _____Attributes result to a single "cause" rather than to multiple causes with varying degrees of probability.

Example:

Multiple factors influence a child's education including, for example, socioeconomic status, neighborhood, and complexity of language used in the home (Berliner & Glass, 2014). These outside-of-school factors appear to be the most significant contributors of "causes" of student achievement.

The relation between student achievement and socioeconomic status was reported from a study of 11,200 school districts across all fifty states. Approximately 200 million reading and mathematics test scores were examined over a five-year time frame. A strong positive correlation was obtained between student achievement and socioeconomic status of students in the district. In general, the higher the socioeconomic status of the school district, the higher the students' achievement. Socioeconomic factors accounted for approximately three-quarters of the variation among achievement between school districts (Reardon, Kalogrides, & Shores, 2017).

The fake news is the assumption that the teacher is the single most important "cause" of student achievement. This assumption is a fundamental flaw and error in value-added models with various methods proposed for teacher accountability. Helping students to attain higher achievement may require more assistance and support from outside-of-school factors.

• _____Does not interpret potential non statistical claims of causation by examining a timeline so that a potential cause came after an event or outcome,
• _____Fake news interprets nonstatistical information as indicating "certainty" for the cause regardless of the source of information, rather than "probable cause" as consistent with the *Federal Rules of Evidence* procedures,
• _____Fake news can present either very large or small numbers to create a different emotional response and interpretation:

Example:

A national debt represented by a huge number of approximately $20 trillion creates a much different response than a small number that indicates interest on the national debt of 1.45% of the gross national product.

Importance of issue:

Different methods of interpreting the information can produce different cognitive and emotional responses that affect our decisions. We may believe or interpret information in many ways; but the obvious fact is that our decisions can have significant consequences.

We need to understand and apply appropriate methods of interpretation of the news. The unfortunate observation is how often the "look for" indicators of misinterpretations in fake news are in our daily news.

The reality is that studies cannot control for all other possible influences upon results and measurement and estimation errors in statistical analysis. These uncontrolled influences and measurement errors mean that we need to interpret any results or claim with a degree of uncertainty or probability rather than as absolute "proof" or "disproof."

We may become more anxious making decisions based upon probability rather than certainty. This is uncomfortable for us, and we often become susceptible to wanting to understand, with certainty, the cause for an event. We often accept the reality of things not seen and accept undocumented or inappropriate information as evidence, if the information promises certainty of understanding. This may predispose us to believe in conspiracy theories—or other false stories—that provide a "definite" or "certain" explanation.

Certainty is an elusive goal. The paradox is that those who believe they are more certain of a cause may have less understanding of other more potentially significant causes.

Inaccurate and fake news often promises certainty—but at what price? The question remains as to how that promise can be true in relation to the many "look for" concerns noted so far in this book. The hope is that each of us will reduce the influence of fake news by interpreting information objectively, rather than subjectively.

Here are some of the most common ways fake news misinterprets information to make a statement with certainty:

• Biased sources of information,
• Contradictory results are not reported,
• Conclusions are only supported with partial information or information from flawed methods or statistical analysis,

- Conclusions based upon a limited or nonrandom sample of persons or events,
- Biased information collection instruments,
- Inappropriate generalization to other groups or to all individuals in a group,
- Lack of control for other possible causes for an event,
- Use of negative evidence argument where burden is upon others to disprove rather than prove a claim (we can't prove it didn't happen),
- Counterfactual argument which explains past events as what "would have happened if,"
- Not reporting a measurement error of scores or an estimation error in predicting scores,
- Constructing a claim to align with personal biases of an intended audience.

Discussion questions:

(1) Have students identify a fake news story that they read. Ask students to identify the specific ways that fake news misinterprets the information in the story.
(2) Ask students to compare the different ways that fake news misinterprets the information and evaluate which way is the most harmful.

Chapter 10

Promises or Recommendations

Measure not by the promises we make, but by the promises we keep.

—Gerald Ford

Why do you not practice what you preach?

—Saint Jerome

Recommendations are often made to influence our behaviors or choices for a particular policy. Promises are given to assure us with certainty of the effectiveness or benefit of the recommendation. Anyone or any group can make promises or recommendations. Which recommendations do we accept and which do we reject? Why?

We have read a kaleidoscope of issues in this book to evaluate the news. Fake news often has false or vague promises or recommendations to influence perceptions and decisions. All recommendations need to be examined to evaluate the feasibility and potential benefits and consequences. Incorrect choices of policies can have a significant effect upon all of us.

This chapter provides some additional indicators to evaluate proposed recommendations. The first checklist has "look for" indicators that provide more credibility that the recommendation is both feasible and potentially effective. The second checklist has "look for" indicators that increase the possibility that the recommendation is not feasible, not effective, and may have unintended or collateral negative results.

Checklist "look for" indicators of more credible recommendations:

- ____Specific information is provided in the recommendation for each of these:
  (1) Financial cost for necessary materials, facilities, and personnel,
  (2) Number of personnel and required training,
  (3) Time frame or schedule of activities and completion,
  (4) Legislative or governmental approval required,
  (5) Measurable indicators to verify outcomes or results,
- ____Specific statement and examples provided of official methods to verify the assumptions supporting the recommendation,
- ____Statement made of specific qualifiers or conditions to a recommended proposal,
- ____Specific and verifiable reasons provided as evidence for why other alternative proposed recommendations are not as effective in cost, feasibility, and/or outcomes,
- ____Verifiable record of promises kept by the source or originator of the recommendation,
- ____Only a single recommendation or proposal is made to avoid an omnibus proposal that combines several and potentially conflicting recommendations.

Checklist "look for" indicators of a fake or less credible recommendation:

- ____Vague or no information provided in the recommendation for any of these:
  (1) Financial cost for necessary materials, facilities, and personnel,
  (2) Number of personnel and required training,
  (3) Time frame or schedule of activities and completion,
  (4) Legislative or governmental approval required,
  (5) Measurable indicators to verify outcomes or results.
- ____Vague or no statement or examples provided of official methods to verify the assumptions supporting the recommendation.

Example:

(1) "Supply side economics" is a phrase and concept used to support an assumption that tax cuts for the wealthy pay for themselves because the wealthy will then invest the tax savings in ways that will provide economic growth for all. A current experiment with this idea is in Kansas where Governor Sam Brownback and the legislature made significant tax cuts. The results after two years of tax cuts are increased deficits in

the state budget, proposals to cut government spending, and economic growth below the national average (Blinder, 2017).

The record from previous attempts for "supply side economics" is inconsistent and generally does not verify or support the assumption that the wealthy will invest and create economic growth that will "trickle down" to all. However, budget deficits and increased disparity between the wealthy and the poor have been the constant results from past attempts.

(2) The Competitive Enterprise Institute (CEI) publishes a yearly document called *The Ten Thousand Commandments* in which estimates are made about financial costs from federal regulations. The document estimates that the cost for 2016 was $1,885,000,000,000.

Specific methods to verify these costs are not provided and the author of the document indicated that the costs of regulation were difficult to quantify as many costs are "indirect" (Crews Jr., 2017). This document makes multiple recommendations for having fewer regulations. Can you guess this document is prepared by an advocacy group?

(3) The United States Office of Management and Budget has calculated financial values of human life. These official values are different for different federal departments with a range between approximately $6 million to $9 million. These values are used to determine the "benefit" when conducting cost-benefit analysis of regulations (McGinty, 2016).

Fake news may use unofficial values or inconsistent values when conducting cost-benefit studies of regulations. What value should be placed upon a life? Should all decisions be based upon a financial cost-benefit analysis? Would the U.S. Chamber of Commerce try to have a different value of human life than proposed by a government agency in conducting cost-benefit analysis?

- _____Vague or no statement made of specific qualifiers or conditions to a recommended proposal,

Example:

Proposals were made at the 2016 Democratic National Convention and by candidate Hillary Clinton for *debt free college for all*. What was not mentioned at that time—but was later offered as a qualifier—was this caveat: debt free college *only* for families with income *below* $125,000.

- _____No verifiable record of promises kept by the source or originator of the recommendation,

Example:

A promise was made to bring jobs back to America because of concerns with immigrants taking jobs from Americans. However, the Mar-A-Lago resort in Florida requested seventy-eight H-2B visas for foreign cooks and housekeepers as temporary workers (Moore, 2016).

The H-2B visa permits foreign workers as guest workers if there are not enough American workers who are "able, willing, qualified, and available to do the work." Is this a promise made, but a promise broken?

• ____No or inaccurate and/or vague reasons are provided for why other alternative proposed recommendations are not as effective in cost, feasibility, and/or outcomes.
• ____Several potentially conflicting recommendations are combined into an omnibus proposal to avoid making a decision about each separate proposal.

Example:

A 2016 Congressional proposal to provide funding for fighting Zika infection (disease caused by bite from a mosquito) also included cuts in funding for Planned Parenthood. This is a "poison pill" where a vote represents conflicting preferences for which a person may not agree with all parts so that supporting one preferred outcome, a person may have to simultaneously support an outcome that is not preferred.

Importance of issue:

We often emotionally respond to promises and then subjectively evaluate the promise based upon our hopes and wishes. As we have repeatedly seen in this book, fake news can promise or make recommendations based upon vague, inaccurate, or even false information.

All of us have responsibility to evaluate the news and any promises or recommendations carefully and objectively. We may need to have objective facts direct our beliefs and decisions.

Some of most basic questions to ask are as follow:

• Is the recommendation feasible regarding the needed resources and legal requirements?
• Is there a direct observable and measurable outcome to determine the success of a recommendation?
• Are any qualifiers or conditions that need to be met or could adversely affect the success of the recommendation?
• Does the individual or organization have a record of making feasible and successful recommendations?

Discussion questions:

(1) Have students "read the fine print" of a recommendation they read or hear in the news. Ask students to list the following: outcomes expected from the recommendation; qualifiers needed for success of the recommendation; past history of success by the person or group making the recommendation; and the feasibility of the recommendation.
(2) Ask students to compare a recommendation with a better alternative recommendation and explain which recommendation is best.

Part IV

HOW FAKE NEWS PERSUADES

Oh, what a tangled web we weave, when first we practice to deceive!

—Sir Walter Scott

This part of the book examines techniques used by fake news to communicate and influence our choices. Chapter 11 presents many ways that fake news deceives us. An example is provided of the dynamics of a conspiracy theory.

Chapter 12 reports that fake news is also within the comments and literature of educational practice. In addition to preparing students to distinguish between real and fake news, educators need to be able to identify fake news that may adversely affect educational practice.

Chapter 11

Techniques of Fake News Communication

He who permits himself to tell a lie once, finds it much easier to do it a second and third time, till at length it becomes habitual.

—Thomas Jefferson

Nature never deceives us; it is always we who deceive ourselves.

—Jean-Jacques Rousseau

Fake news can spread as fast as a wildfire carried on the winds of social media distribution. Unchecked, fake news can burn and destroy our society.

Previous chapters have indicated multiple issues that have supported the creation and distribution of fake news. We have seen significant four hurdles that may prevent us from controlling the spread of fake news:

- Finding accurate available information,
- Our limited knowledge of ways to evaluate the news,
- Our own biases in filtering the news,
- Our lack of commitment to seek accurate news.

Multiple "look for" indicators were presented to help us to distinguish real from fake news. Representative and real-world examples of fake and inaccurate news information were included to illustrate the inaccuracies that are part of fake news, and, are part of our everyday lives.

The questions remain about the processes and techniques by which fake news persuades and influences. Understanding those processes and techniques may help each of us—and our students—to become more resilient to the allure of fake news.

This chapter describes multiple techniques used to deceive, spread, and influence our thoughts and choices. A few of these techniques have been reported in previous chapters. It is challenging to present the extensive list of all of the techniques used in fake news. An alphabetical list of commonly used techniques is described with some selected real-life examples.

The startling observation is fake news uses real techniques. These techniques are used in everyday living and in social media, print, radio, and television. The techniques are even used in press conferences or interviews.

Sun-tzu, an ancient Chinese military writer, observed, "A military operation involves deception." If we are engaged in the war against fake news, then these techniques of communication may be called "weapons of mass deception."

- Accuse. Fake news will accuse the other person or organization of the inappropriate behavior the source of the fake news is doing,

Example:

Do we ever accuse someone of bias because they do not agree with our bias? Do politicians sometimes provide fake news to the media, but then accuse the media of creating fake news?

- Anonymous or un-sourced claim. Fake news can claim the use of anonymous sources to avoid providing a method to verify a statement.

NOTE: Anonymity may be necessary in some reporting to protect the individual source. A balance is necessary between protecting the identity of an anonymous source in order to obtain sensitive information—and the need to verify the accuracy of information.

Using anonymous sources has greater credibility if additional information is provided such as detailing events that confirms or substantiates a claim. If an anonymous source is used, then a disclaimer should so indicate and provide as much additional information as possible to support the statement, such as information from "a source at the White House" or "a source in the State Department."

Example:

Many have condemned the practice of anonymity as citations for news stories. However, a White House communications aide asked officials to speak, on the condition of anonymity, to challenge reports on presidential campaign contacts with Russia (Miller & Entous, 2017).

- Attack the facts. Fake news attacks the facts of others as inaccurate even if the fake news cannot verify the facts, and may try to substitute alternative facts,

Example:

The use of the term "alternative facts" as a means to substitute alternative information has been widely used. A prominent example is the estimated crowd at presidential inauguration. Photographic evidence facts were attacked as inaccurate and that alternative facts support the claim of a larger crowd.

- Attack the question. Fake news attacks the question as being irrelevant or inappropriate in order to avoid an answer.
- Attack the questioner. Fake news attacks the person or organization asking questions in order to draw attention away from answering or revealing personal or logical weakness of a position (sometimes called character assassination).

Example:

Here is a comment made to reporters at a press conference: "You know, you're dishonest people."

- Avoid an answer. Fake news will avoid giving an answer with expectation that the question will be forgotten or the attention will shift to another topic.
- Biased sources. Fake news will use information from a biased source such as a think tank or advocacy group without indication of the methods used by those groups to obtain or analyze the information.
- Blame others for personal mistakes. Fake news will blame others for inaccurate information.

Example:

An inaccurate statement was made about the margin of the electoral victory in the last presidential election. After questioning, the mistake was blamed on others with this comment: "I was given that information."

- Blame the victim. Fake news will distract by blaming the victim for an event.

Example:

The Democratic National Committee has often been blamed for being hacked by the Russians rather than the Russians being blamed for the hacking.

- Certainty. Fake news will make statements that claim a certainty of "proof" or "disproof" of a claim, rather than probability, as many persons have a bias for certainty.
- Change or redirect topic. Fake news will change or redirect the discussion or communication to a different topic to avoid addressing the initial topic or focusing upon a topic of particular interest.
- Cherry picking. Fake news will only answer or respond to a part of a question or to a particular individual.
- Confirmation bias. Fake news is effective if supporting or confirming what an intended audience already believes.
- Conspiracy theory. Fake news will offer a theory or explanation about a secret plan of others or other organizations or events.

Example:

The myth that the measles, mumps, and rubella (MMR) vaccine causes autism has been consistently found to be inaccurate; but a theory still exists of a vast conspiracy of groups to inflict autism through vaccinations (Specter, 2017). Comments supporting the connection between MMR vaccinations and autism continue to be made in political debates (Hotez, 2017).

- Counterfactual argument. Fake news will give an illogical reply when defending a claim about an event by stating "you can't disprove that" or "you can't prove it didn't happen." If so, then assume this proves supporting the claim.
- Deflection. Fake news will attack the media or the messenger, so cast doubt upon credibility and distract from other issues.

Example:

The statements about the news media as an enemy of the "people" are too numerous to list. The important point is the effort to discredit media that might provide contrary, but factual, information,

- Delay giving answer. Fake news delays giving an answer in order to have the issue forgotten or to have time to develop an alternative story.

Example:

Here is a statement we often hear: "Let me get back to you."

• Denial. Fake news will deny an event or making a statement or a claim.

Example:

A classic way to use denial is this statement when confronted: "I was just joking." This denial is often combined with blaming the other person for misunderstanding ("gaslighting").

• Disclaim. Fake news will claim that others are asking the question or have the issue. ("I'm just putting it out there" or "people have been talking" or "it isn't me.")
• Doubt. Fake news tries to create doubt about other claims or explanations.
• Fabricate information. Fake news will make up numbers, data, and/or results without verification of sources or methods.

Example:

The claim of 3 million illegals voting in the presidential election has widely been debunked as verification of this claim has not been produced.

• False conclusion. Fake news will make a false conclusion or interpretation from a document to change focal points.

Example:

Previously noted in this book is the claim that the ODNI report indicated that Russian hacking did not change the election results. The ODNI report did not address that issue and only indicated hacking did not affect the voting machines (Office of the Director of National Intelligence, 2017).

• False equivalence. Fake news will attempt to avoid responsibility for a result or action by falsely stating that everyone or every organization does it.

Example:

An interviewer made a statement that Vladimir Putin was a "killer." His interviewee replied: "We've got killers. What do you think—our country is so innocent?" (Davidson, 2017). Is this false equivalence startling?

- Fear. Fake news will attempt to create an emotional response of fear as fearful readers or viewers are less likely critically to evaluate the accuracy of fake news.

Example:

Judge James Robart denied an executive order regarding a travel ban from certain countries. The response to this decision claimed the judge put the country in peril and: "If something happens, blame him." (Davidson, 2017).

- Frame (reframe) the question or issue. Fake news will establish the questions or issues or structure the question or issue to direct toward a desired conclusion.
- "Gaslighting." Fake news will attempt to cast doubt upon the perceptions of others and may state that other persons or organizations misunderstand or misperceive.
- General or vague answers. Fake news will give nonspecific and vague answers or promises as the vagueness provides enough room to not be held accountable for any results or accuracy and without providing materials or documents to permit verification of claims.
- Hyperbole (Hope). Fake news will exaggerate a claim or result (truthful hyperbole) to increase a sense of hope and gain support for the claim.
- Hypothetical. Fake news will suggest hypothetical or possible explanations to investigate ("have you looked into" or "have you considered?") to create doubt.
- Labeling (positive). Fake news may assign a characteristic to a person or group with a challenge to live up to that characteristic label ("we know you are kind and will support this issue").
- Multiple and rapid claims. Fake news will make multiple claims without allowing sufficient time to evaluate the accuracy of one claim before presenting another claim (distracts from close examination of each issue).
- Provoke. Fake news will provoke an accuser so they act in emotional ways consistent with ways they are portrayed (need to avoid responding in inappropriate language or with nonprofessional reporting or actions to confirm the accusation).
- Repeat. Fake news repeats and repeats a term or claim with the expectation that the term or claim will be accepted by others after repeated exposure.
- Restrict access. Fake news will have restricted access to the presenters or opportunities to ask questions for clarification.
- Social proof. Fake news will claim that many support the claim or statement, and this indicates the accuracy of the claim. However, automated

"bots" can create an increase in the number of responses to distort the number supporting a claim.

- "Straw man." Fake news will create a fictitious claim about a person or group as an enemy or adversarial force and direct energy toward that "straw person" to blame for problems.

Examples:

"The government,"
"The mainstream media,"
"The media,"

- Trial balloon. Fake news will make a claim or statement (usually anonymously), just to see reaction before claiming support.
- Urgency. Fake news often will indicate an urgency or a need to act or to disseminate to others without sufficient time to evaluate the information.

As we can see, many techniques are used to create and spread fake news. Examining and understanding the dynamics of creation and communication may assist each of us to become resistant to the effects of fake news.

The techniques listed above are only part of the equation. Fake news sometimes wins the war against truth because of the difficulties we face in trying to jump the four hurdles mentioned earlier in this book:

- Available information;
- Limited understanding of objective methods of evaluation;
- Our biases;
- Uncertain commitment to apply objective methods in evaluating the news.

The checklist "look for" indicators included in this book provides opportunities to increase understanding of methods objectively to evaluate and distinguish real and fake news. Fake news receives a quick death by an informed citizenry. Unfortunately, fake news thrives in an environment in which subjectivity and bias supersede objective reasoning and analysis.

Many decisions in life are based more upon unconscious factors than with conscious reason. Multiple investigators have found that our beliefs and biases, once formed, are difficult to change even when presented with objective contradictory evidence (Kolbert, 2017).

Heuristics of confirmation bias, denial, overconfidence, and others described earlier support our current belief system by seeking confirming evidence and rejecting contrary evidence to our beliefs. These heuristics make us more likely to perceive and interpret information in particular ways that make it more likely that we will believe fake news and conspiracy theories.

The rapid speed and the urgency to disseminate fake news provide little time for slow and careful objective analysis of the news. We feel an exhilaration and excitement when we discover any news that confirms our bias. We then become more convinced of the truth of our beliefs and are more likely to share quickly the message with others rather than use a "slow" or more analytic examination of the news (Kahneman, 2011).

This overconfidence bias indicates that we may be simultaneously certain of our understanding and the correctness of our beliefs. We may then subjectively—rather than objectively—evaluate the news. A consequence is we may then be more susceptible to fake news and conspiracy theories that offer an explanation or a "cause" for events that confirm our biases.

One of the most common and difficult to dismiss of the techniques of fake news is the conspiracy theory. The conspiracy theory is assumed to be a secret plan to commit a subversive or illegal act against others or other organizations without their knowledge or agreement.

Many conspiracy theories exist. Why do these conspiracy theories exist and how to do become accepted by some of us? A conspiracy theory is able to be accepted by some of us because the theory provides a certainty of explanation or "cause" that aligns with our biases. The conspiracy theory only requires "fast" or subjective thinking without the need to "slowly" do objective thinking of all evidence.

Four predominant characteristics of conspiracy theories are:

- A pattern of events is presented, but not necessarily connected in a causal manner with a chain of events in a timeline.
- "Straw men" of secret agents or organizations of the conspiracy are attributed to have power to "cause" the events.
- Supporters of conspiracies are overconfident of understanding, refuse to consider other explanations, and reject any disconfirming objective evidence.
- Supporters of conspiracies often use a counterfactual argument previously described in this book by which the burden of proof is upon others to disprove the conspiracy (difficult when a secret force is involved). If others cannot disprove, then they claim the theory must be correct.

Objective analysis of evidence permits debunking a conspiracy theory. However, as we can see, it is difficult for some individuals to accept objective information that questions a conspiracy theory. These individuals are confident in knowledge of the cause.

Here is an example of a conspiracy theory that was found to be fake news, but is starting to regain distribution as a conspiracy:

Example:

Dr. Andrew Wakefield published a study in England in which the claim was made of the MMR vaccine "causing" autism. That study was found to be fraudulent with inclusion of falsified data from a small sample of children. Dr. Wakefield lost his medical license for ethical violations in conducting and reporting falsified research. The results of Dr. Wakefield's study have been debunked and never been confirmed by other researchers.

The logical assumption would be that the MMR vaccine does not cause autism. Today, many parents and even a television celebrity host continue to accept Dr. Wakefield's false conclusion and have refused to vaccinate their children. No link between vaccination and autism has been reported by the Centers for Disease Control and Prevention (Schipani, 2017).

The conspiracy is believed to be a secret agreement of the government and pharmaceutical companies to inject autism into society to have increased profits from prescribing medicines to treat autism (Specter, 2017). The conspiracy theory of MMR vaccinations and autism has significant consequences for all of us. As a historical note, more original native inhabitants of the Americas died from exposure to measles than from all of the battles fought with settlers. Measles still kills approximately 100,000 children each year across the world (Hotez, 2017).

What will happen if more parents refuse to vaccinate their children because of a false conspiracy theory? Will failure to vaccinate contribute to increased rates of measles? The answer to these questions is that measles cases are more frequent where families refuse vaccination (Chabris & Simons, 2010).

Conspiracy theories can be promoted for personal, political, and even financial reasons. Fake news organizations—radio and television commentators and other media—can receive more traffic and advertising revenue from posting "click bait" headlines of secret conspiracies. Our curiosity makes us want to check this potentially exciting new revelation about a secret conspiracy.

We all love to hear "secrets." Don't believe that we want to find out the "secret"? Here is a secret we have been reluctant to share with others, but now feel an obligation to do so even if we suffer some consequence.

As we probably know, the government has been engaged is a secret conspiracy to control public broadcast media to promote their hidden agenda. Hidden messages in commercials and advertising have tried to influence us to accept the control of the media as a populist way to represent real American values. If you skip to page 243, you will find the identity of the secret group behind this conspiracy. Please be careful not to reveal their identity as they have powerful ways to affect you.

A frightening situation is simply the prevalence of conspiracy theories in our everyday lives. How many can you identify? How many current conspiracy theories will be explained when better evidence becomes available? How would we determine that a conspiracy theory is a fake news story?

By the way, did we skip ahead to page 243 to find the identity of the secret group? Page 243 is not in this book. Are we all susceptible to the allure of a conspiracy theory?

Importance of issue.

This chapter presented numerous techniques and examples by which fake news is created and used. Fake news exists in many situations that we encounter in everyday living and in information we read or hear.

Regardless if the fake news is with words, numbers, or visual information, the consequence is the same. Fake news can harm all of us. We make decisions that can affect the freedoms and liberties for which our Founding Father gave their lives. Fake news can also contribute to making decisions with deadly consequences.

Understanding how to objectively distinguish real and fake news is a theme throughout this book. Helping students become better prepared to evaluate the news is an important goal for all educators. The benefit to society for all of us cannot be overestimated.

Every profession may be influenced by inaccurate and fake news. Presentation of some selected myths and fake news in educational practice in this next chapter is intended to increase awareness of educators that fake news is not just confined to politics, advertising, or other professions. Educational practice is no exception to the bad influence of fake news.

Discussion questions:

(1) Have students identify and share fake news stories that they hear, read, or see. Ask them to identify the specific techniques used to create and spread the fake news.
(2) Have students provide a reason why the different techniques of creating and spreading fake news is effective.

Chapter 12

Fake News About Education

The very spring and root of honesty and virtue lie in good education.

—Plutarch

Truth persuades by teaching, but does not teach by persuading.

—Tertullian

Educators are not immune to the influence of inaccurate or even fake ideas or news. How many times have educators been told that previous practices and instructional strategies are no longer appropriate? Were previous recommendations a fake? How do we know that the "latest research" provides better recommendations?

Educational practice has also been affected by a multitude of unintentionally inaccurate news supported by poorly designed research studies. Just pause for a moment and reflect upon all of the different practices that educators have applied and then rejected. How many of these practices were judged to be so important, but the importance has diminished? Here are just a few of these recent practices (Paul & Elder, 2007): self-esteem movement, whole language instruction, and character education. What evidence would suggest that these practices are no longer as important? Here are some school practices from a more distant past that are now widely rejected:

• Corporal punishment,
• Rote memorization,
• Extensive homework every night,

- Special education students should be in separate classes,
- Girls should be discouraged from taking mathematics courses.

We may laugh or cry, but those were once common educational practices.

Do educators often feel that it is difficult to distinguish between real and fake recommendations for educational practices? If so, then we can better appreciate the perspective of students who may have similar difficulty in distinguishing the real from the fake and may simply find it easier to accept easily available fake ideas or news.

Poorly designed research studies are an annoyance in trying to identify appropriate educational practices. Does it seem that every year there is something "new" from research findings? These new findings are often just the correction or further elaboration of unintentional errors in previous research.

A more difficult and ominous concern is the intentional creation and dissemination of fake news about educational practices. Cheating on tests to raise test scores and manipulating the overall grade or the rating given to a school are only a few of the ways that fake news has been used to deceive the public. In fact, school administrators in several districts have been found guilty of cheating to raise test scores.

Fake news within a particular school district about test scores is an unprofessional practice, but generally confined to particular school districts. A broader application of fake news is the criticism of the American public education system.

Free public education is considered as an important mechanism supporting our democracy and helping students to develop as informed and productive citizens. The public schools have provided opportunities for everyone to climb the ladder of success.

The U. S. Department of Education (1983), however, stated that American schools were mediocre and that public schools were failing adequately to teach students. The notion that public schools have failed America has grown as an organized movement.

Constructive suggestions to improve the educational system will always be useful. However, fake news and inaccurate information have been used to support this criticism of the public school system (Ravitch, 2013). The criticisms are often attacks that may have underlying financial, sociological, or racial reasons.

A financial reason is obvious. Annual expenditures on the American education system are nearing $1 trillion. Might some corporations look upon this amount of expenditures as an opportunity to make money? Here are some questions to consider on why financial reasons might tempt corporations or other organizations and individuals to criticize the public school system:

- Could corporations see business opportunities to generate profits in establishing alternatives to public education?
- Could some public tax dollars be directed toward these alternatives to provide a secure base of revenue?
- Could profits be even greater if traditional bargaining rights of school employees are reduced, and employees are replaced with others at a lower wage scale and with fewer benefits and protections?
- Could the alternative be marketed as offering "choice"?
- Could profits be even greater if the alternatives to public education have either reduced or no standards of accountability for showing results—or better outcomes?

Guess what the answer is to each of those questions. The answer is, of course, yes.

Sociological or racial reasons for criticizing the public schools are more subtle. Can fake news be created to support some children's attending schools that are not economically or racially integrated?

Corporate interest to secure profits and the opportunities for some to send children to alternative educational opportunities that minimize potential school integration may be intentional foundations for many of the criticisms and fake news of educational practice (Berliner & Glass, 2014). Do we believe that observation?

Here are a few of the fifty prevalent criticisms of the public educational system reported by Berliner and Glass (2014). Can we identify any suspected financial corporate interests or sociological reasons for supporting alternatives to avoid attending integrated public schools?

- Teacher unions are responsible for much poor school performance.
- Charter schools are better than traditional public schools.
- Class size does not matter.
- Teachers in the United States are unionized and well-paid.
- Private schools are better than public schools.
- Tuition tax credits help poor children escape failing public schools.
- Preschool and kindergarten programs are not worth the investment.

We could continue to elaborate upon this list, as we see so many criticisms. Have we heard any? Do we have a belief about the accuracy of each of those above criticisms?

The topic of "school choice" is increasingly being discussed as an educational policy. Arguments for and against school choice are actively debated. Let's take a look at those arguments and assumptions.

The rationale for "school choice" appears to rest upon several assumptions:

- Ideological assumption that everyone should have freedom of choice without government interference to avoid a "nanny state."
- Everyone is capable of making choices in their own best interest and better than choices made by others.
- Assertions by economist Milton Friedman and others that choice and competition are the best ways to improve schools (Thaler & Sunstein, 2009).
- Recent statements by President Trump and others to equate school choice as a "civil rights issue"—by which school vouchers permit children from poor families to have choice—would have the same rights to a quality education as children from wealthy families (Superville & Lemire, 2017).

The rationale against "school choice" rests upon several assumptions:

- Funding will diminish for public schools and will adversely affect the quality of educational services that can be provided.
- Voucher programs to attend charter and private schools are taxpayer dollars and with little transparency in how that money is spent.
- Charter, online, and private and religious schools often do not have public accountability for reporting what students have learned and been tested.
- The voucher programs and the charter schools are an attempt to turn education into a competitive, profit-making business.
- The voucher program may be a subsidy for wealthy families who can already afford to send their children to private and religious K-12 schools.
- The voucher program is a subtle form of racial and socioeconomic discrimination in that only the poor and minority students will be left in the public education.

Do we see any difficulties in trying to resolve the issue? As we can observe, many assumptions for and against school choice can be easily and widely made.

What should be the role of objectively collecting verifiable facts in making a decision about school choice? What facts do we all need? Are facts optional and do we just make a decision based upon our biases or opportunities? Can we set aside our biases and objectively evaluate the news about school choice?

What can educators do in response to criticisms of educational practice? Educators need to develop skills for objectively evaluating the news. The hope is that all educators will be able to apply the checklist "look for" indicators included in this book to evaluate news of educational practices and outcomes.

Discussion questions:

(1) Have students identify and share fake news stories of educational programs or practices that they hear, read, or see. Ask them to identify the specific "look for" indicators that suggest the news story is fake and/or misleading.
(2) Have students provide a reason why groups were creating and spreading fake news about educational programs or practices.

Part V

PREVENTING FAKE NEWS FROM SPREADING

If there is anything that we wish to change in the child, we should first examine it and see whether it is not something that could better be changed in ourselves.

—Carl Jung

Preventing fake news from influencing our personal and civic decisions is the focus of the three chapters in this part of the book. All of us have an interest in making the best possible decisions.

Chapter 13 presents some strategies that each of us may individually apply. The knowledge and skills provided in this book with checklist "look for" indicators are a foundation for individually and objectively examining the news. We must also minimize our biases and have a commitment to have objectively verifiable facts guide our decisions.

Chapter 14 includes some instructional strategies that teachers may find helpful in planning learning experiences for students. A lesson plan, project-based learning experience, and a fun game of fake news bingo may all stimulate the imagination of teachers for additional meaningful activities to help students to beat fake news.

Chapter 15 discusses activities that may be considered in our society to safeguard against fake news. As we have seen, fake news is prevalent in many areas of our everyday living. Our legacy is to prepare our children to distinguish what is real from fake in their lives. Our future society may depend upon how well we prepare our children.

Chapter 13

Protecting Against Fake News

A wise skepticism is the first attribute of a good critic.

—James Russell Lowell

It is a double pleasure to deceive the deceiver.

—Jean de La Fontaine

All of us have biases that affect our perceptions about the reality of the world as is and the way we want. How we process information is influenced by our biases, knowledge, skills, and dispositions in evaluating the news.

We wonder, "Will I be able objectively to evaluate the news?" The four hurdles mentioned earlier are significant obstacles.

The hope is that we have now gained additional information to objectively evaluate the available information and distinguish real from fake news. As noted earlier, available guides and resources to assist educators in preparing students to evaluate the news primarily focus upon media literacy or determining the accuracy of sources of news. This focus is insufficient. Guides and instruction also needed to assist in developing data literacy and critical thinking skills.

Here are some topics that we included in this book to develop necessary knowledge and skills to evaluate the news more comprehensively and objectively:

- Know where to look for accurate sources,
- Know the language and terms,
- Know how much information is sufficient,
- Know how methods of collecting information influence the news,

- Know what type of information is relevant,
- Know how to analyze the information,
- Know how to interpret and understand the information,
- Know how to check promised recommendations with reality,
- Know how fake news deceives,
- Know fake news regarding educational practice,
- Know how to protect against the influence of fake news (this chapter),
- Know instructional methods to assist students to distinguish real and fake news,
- Know educational policies to safeguard from fake news.

Knowing how objectively to evaluate the news is not sufficient. The "landscape of our mind" may be used to describe the most important territory in human geography. However, the geography of our thought processes is often influenced by the destructive storms of emotion and bias.

Two challenging obstacles remain for each of us. The first is to reflect upon and minimize our own biases in evaluating the news. The second is the commitment to apply objective and factual information in making decisions, even if the facts indicate we need to change our decision.

Examining our biases requires us to become aware of our tendencies for "fast" and subjective thinking that permits us quickly to process and respond to the news. We look for patterns even in meaningless events. A cause, even if secretive and nearly invisible, is often attributed to the event. We need to "slow" our thinking to permit more careful and objective evaluation of the news.

Remember our description of conspiracy theories in a previous chapter? When we hear a suspected conspiracy theory, here are some objective steps to evaluate and determine if the theory is more likely to be fake news (Shermer, 2011):

- No evidence provided of the causal connection or timeline between events,
- Individuals or organizations of the conspiracy are attributed to have significant power to cause the events,
- The greater the potential number of people involved in the conspiracy, the less likely they can remain silent about the secret and preserve the "secret" plan,
- The greater the scale of the plan to entire countries or world domination, the less likely the theory is to be true,
- The fewer the verifiable facts, the less likely the theory is to be true,
- The more the theory supporters reject any contrary evidence, the less likely the theory is to be true.

Developing more reflective and critical thinking skills may also help students to minimize biases. Here are some relevant strategies developed by the Central Intelligence Agency (CIA) that can support a more objective analysis of information in the news (Newberg & Waldman, 2006):

- Examining alternative points of view,
- Thinking backward to try and explain how a future event might have occurred,
- Assume a different interpretation and try to examine assumptions that support that alternative assumption,
- List assumptions supporting a current interpretation,
- Ask questions,
- Double-check supposed facts.

Some earlier suggestions and questions from this book are also useful for objectively evaluating the news from different media:

- Doubt every source of news,
- Seek independent additional sources of news,
- Question all new information,
- Understand the specific terms,
- Consider alternative explanations,
- Follow an objective method to evaluate all news to answer questions (checklist "look for" items can assist with an objective method),
- Is the information accurate and verifiable?
- Is the information relevant or appropriate?
- Is there enough or sufficient information?
- Become aware and minimize personal biases in analysis and interpretation of the news,
- Objective and verifiable facts should direct your decisions,
- Make decisions with knowledge of probability rather than absolute "proof" or "disproof,"
- Be willing to change your decisions as more accurate, relevant, and complete information becomes available.

Fake news and false knowledge can have deadly consequences. The *Titanic* is not just the title of a movie, but was a ship that was assumed to be "unsinkable." The ship did sink on its first trip with the loss of over 1,000 lives.

Here is another list of practical suggestions offered for us to be skeptical of all information in our search for distinguishing real and fake news as the fake news may have deadly consequences (Burns, 2008):

- Be aware of news that first creates a strong emotion. Emotion may lead to evaluate the news subjectively rather than objectively.
- Be careful of the "framing" or use of language and terms that may create distorted "narrative" explanation of a proposal. This is particularly evident with ambiguous words such as "patriotic," "traditional," and others.
- Be careful and examine the evidence and the ways that the evidence was collected. Evidence collected from biased samples and methodology is often at the heart of fake news.
- Be careful of statements simply because the statement is often repeated. Repetition does not guarantee accuracy or truth.
- Be careful of who endorses a proposal or the news. Seek independent and multiple sources to avoid the bias from advocacy groups or those sources motivated to spread fake news.
- Be careful of those sources stating a certainty of "proof" or "disproof." Most situations in life offer the possibility of multiple causes. The best suggestion is to seek sources that offer a statement of probability and acknowledgment of potential other causes rather than a certainty of a single cause.

On a personal level, we may want to avoid directly responding to a falsehood or to fake news. Directly confronting and saying that a statement is false is sometimes counterproductive. Individuals will not be receptive and will deny or avoid responding. Directly challenging the accuracy of the statements of another person is not a way to make friends, but is a fantastic way to make enemies.

Our minds sometimes work in mysterious ways. If we directly confront a falsehood or fake claim, then we actually strengthen the falsehood. Doesn't this sound illogical? Here is why this results. Confronting the falsehood increases attention and recognition of the false or fake claim. The other person will also dismiss your statement and, therefore, feel increasingly confident of the "truth" of its falsehood or fake news. This process also has neurological involvement as contradictory information activates brain regions responsible for emotional reactions (Lehrer, 2009).

We have several choices of how to respond. One choice is to just ignore the fake news if we feel the falsehood is an attempt to divert attention, "frame" a discussion, or move argument away from a more important topic. This attempt to divert is an effective strategy for politicians as journalists often "take the bait," will try to "fact check" the falsehood, and divert their attention away from other issues.

The politician often is aware of the falsehood or fake news, but the strategy is effective. The examples in chapter 11 from a press conference are illustrative of an attempt to shift attention away from some issues.

A second choice is to go through a process of having the person who states a falsehood describe the reasons and evidence for the false or fake claim. We might ask the person to do so to "help us to understand." Persons are very willing to explain their falsehoods or fake claims because individuals believe they can convince us of the "truth of their fake news." Here are the steps in this process to help us to "understand":

1) Ask for their explanation so we can better understand,
2) State you could be wrong, so the explanation will improve your understanding of how their suggestion or claim works,
3) Validate their feelings by indicating how we both want a suggestion to make things better,
4) Ask for explanations to help understand and, if possible, any demonstrations or evidence,
5) Ask for any ideas from them about limitations of how their suggestion might not work,
6) Ask for any ideas of how other explanations or suggestions would or would not work,
7) Ask for examples.

Here is why this second choice is the best to confront someone with a false or fake claim. Many times, the person with the fake claim will recognize some of the limitations and problems of their fake news when they have to explain how it "works." This person may then be less defensive if he or she then have at least an element of doubt of the accuracy of their fake news.

We are also influenced by others. In fact, we have a sense of "bonding" with others when we rapidly forward messages from social media. We need carefully to examine what we forward to others. Do we have any responsibility to our friends for the accuracy of the information we send to them? Do they have any responsibility to us?

We encourage others to take some time to check the information. What would we feel if someone sent fake news to our friends and they made a bad decision as they acted upon that news? How do we feel if we act upon fake news? Treat others as we want to be treated is a universal idea.

As we see, knowledge and skills distinguishing real and fake news are not enough. We have to follow a process to think about the information in ways that may be contrary to our assumptions. We need to set aside our biases and follow objectively factual information even if it means that we need to change our decisions.

In addition to our mind, we need the moral courage from our heart and determination and commitment from within to win the war against fake news. Hope we are now better prepared.

Discussion questions:

(1) Have students identify three techniques they can use to prevent being influenced by fake news.
(2) Ask students to evaluate and share in group discussion the best ways to avoid being influenced by fake news.

Chapter 14

Instructional Activities

The direction in which education starts a man will determine his future life.

—Plato

A teacher affects eternity: he can never tell where his influence stops.

—Henry Adams

This chapter provides some examples of different instructional activities that a teacher may consider for assisting students to gain knowledge of methods and indicators to distinguish real from fake news. The possibilities for many other and varied instructional activities are endless. The examples included here are only representative of some of these activities.

The first activity is a sample of a lesson/unit plan prepared by a teacher using the universal form of a lesson plan (Wiggins & McTighe, 2005). The categories of instructional tasks and supplemental resources are included.

The second activity is a project-based inquiry of investigating a real-world problem. Students can apply the knowledge they have gained in distinguishing real from fake news about the problem. Students will also have opportunities for higher order thinking skills of evaluating the news and proposing evidence-based recommendations for solutions to the problem.

The third activity is a fake news bingo game. The intent of this activity is to provide practice in identifying indicators of fake news and communication of fake news in the real world.

ACTIVITY (1) SAMPLE LESSON/UNIT PLAN

Created by: Mary Erste, English Teacher
      Strongsville High School, Strongsville, Ohio
Mini-Unit: "Fake News: What Is it and How Can Students Detect It?"

STAGE 1: IDENTIFY DESIRED RESULTS

Established goals (G):

- Students will discuss the concept of fake news as a problem for society and media.
- Students will recognize the use of fake news techniques in current media.
- Students will use the vocabulary and terms concerning fake news to express ideas.
- Students will discuss these concepts in small differentiated intentional groups.
- Students will produce a graphic organizer to represent ideas.

  Central Focus: Identifying fake news tactics as they are used in news stories through discussion and activities.

Enduring understandings (U):

Students will understand that. . .

- Fake news is difficult but not impossible to discern from real news.
- Many stories include real information which makes the inaccuracy difficult to discern.
- Specific strategies can be used to determine if a news article is fake or real.

ISTE technology standards for students:

- 3.b Locate, organize, analyze, evaluate, synthesize, and ethically use information from a variety of sources and media
- 4.b Plan and manage activities to develop a solution or complete a project

Essential questions (Q):

Students will strive to answer. . .

- Why would news be faked?
- How is news classified as fake?
- What motivates the use of fake news?
- Who controls the media and dissemination of information?

Misconceptions:

- These ideas are not solely based on unreliable sources or lack of credibility.
- Fake news is not always easy to spot.
- Fake news will affect our culture's media literacy in the future.

Students will know (K):

- The relationship between fake news and manipulation of language.
- The process of media consumption.
- When a message is exaggerated or the meaning is changed by hyperbole.
- The definition of a variety of the attached terms.

Academic language:

- (see the list of fake news techniques in table 14.1).
- Media consumption.
- Deception.

Table 14.1. Fake news techniques

Fake News Techniques	*Definition*
1. Accuse	accuse the other person of inappropriate behavior
2. Anonymous sources	identity of source is not stated
3. Attack the facts	attacks the facts of others as inaccurate even if the fake news cannot verify the facts, and may try to substitute alternative facts
4. Attack the question	attack the question as being irrelevant or inappropriate
5. Attack the questioner	draw attention away from answering or revealing personal or logical weakness
6. Avoid an answer	no answer to question with expectation that question will be forgotten or attention shifts to another topic
7. Biased sources	information obtained from an advocacy group without indication of methods used to obtain information,
8. Blame others for personal mistakes	others are blamed for mistakes
9. Blame the victim	blame victim for a problem to distract or distance personal responsibility,
10. Certainty	certainty of "proof" or "disproof" of claim, rather than probability
11. Change or redirect topic	try to change topic to avoid providing an answer
12. Cherry picking	answer or respond to a part of a question or to a particular individual
13. Confirmation bias	supporting or confirming what an intended audience already believes
14. Conspiracy theory	offer an explanation about a secret plan

(Continued)

Table 14.1. (Continued)

Fake News Techniques	*Definition*
15. Counterfactual argument	"you can't disprove that" or "you can't prove it didn't happen"
16. Deflection	attack the messenger or other sources to cast doubt and distract from the issue
17. Delay giving answer	delay an answer to have time to develop an alternative story or time for issue to be forgotten
18. Denial	deny making a statement or an action
19. Disclaim	claim that others are asking the question or raising the issue
20. Doubt	create uncertainty about a statement, conclusion, or explanation
21. Fabricate information	make up data or results without verification of sources
22. False conclusion	fake news will make a false conclusion or interpretation from a document to change focal points
23. False equivalence	avoid responsibility for significance of an action by claiming that everyone else does the same
24. Fear	fake news will attempt to create an emotional response of fear as fearful readers or viewers are less likely to critically evaluate the accuracy of fake news
25. Frame or reframe the question or issue	structure or pose the question in a manner to "lead" or influence the answer
26. "Gaslighting" cast doubt	cast doubt upon the perceptions of others and state they did not understand or they are too sensitive
27. General or vague answers	nonspecific answers using conditional or tentative terms
28. Hyperbole	make exaggerated claims to heighten the sense of hope
29. Hypothetical	suggest alternative explanations to investigate, to create doubt, and distract
30. Labeling positive	assign a characteristic to a person or group with a challenge to live up to that characteristic label
31. Multiple and rapid claims	make multiple claims without allowing sufficient time to evaluate the accuracy of one claim before presenting another claim (distracts from close examination of each issue)
32. Provoke	antagonize an accuser with the hope the accuser acts in an emotional manner
33. Repeat	state a claim multiple times with the expectation that repetition will increase acceptance of the claim
34. Restrict access	data or persons are not made available for asking questions or clarification
35. Social proof	claim that a statement or conclusion must be correct because many people support the conclusion
36. "Straw men"	create a fictitious claim about a person or group as an enemy or adversarial force and direct energy toward that "straw person" to blame for problems
37. Trial balloon	make a claim or statement (usually anonymously) just to see reaction before claiming support or not
38. Urgency	pressure to quickly act without time to evaluate the information

Students will be able to (S):

- Read and comprehend a story from a provided fake news source.
- Apply the checklist to identify the fake news tactics used within the given story.
- Discuss leveled depth of knowledge questions in small groups.
- Explain the connection and similarities to classmates in full class discussion.

Materials/resources:

- Passages from fake news articles.
- Passages from actual news articles.
- Column from PBS.org for warm-up activity.
- Notes on fake news tactics.
- Fake news indicators handout.
- Headlines and passages worksheet.
- Exit Slip question.

STAGE 2: DETERMINE EVIDENCE FOR ASSESSING LEARNING

Performance task(s) (T) (aka: SA):

1. Day 1: Students will be able to name and explain three fake news techniques on an exit slip.
2. Day 2: Students will be able to identify two of the three fake news techniques used in the given source.

Other evidence (OE) (aka: PA/FA)

1. Teacher observation and anecdotal notes on rubric during small group discussion.
2. Day 1: Fake news headline will be checked in a class and answers will be recorded.
3. Day 2: Depth of knowledge questions will be assessed for accuracy.
4. Day 2: Extension of discussion for homework.

STAGE 3: BUILD LEARNING PLAN

Learning activities (L):

Day 1:

1. (Hook/Pre-Assessment) "Column—most teens can't tell fake from real news" by Sam Wineberg and Sarah McGrew from PBS.org, December 13, 2016.

a. Determine the author's main message.

b. Review: what is fake news? What makes something fake?

2. Teacher Led Instruction: Notes on fake news techniques (see attached materials).

a. Students take individual notes on ten main ideas.

b. Students each receive a fake news indicators handout.

3. Pair Activity: Students will be introduced to current fake news through a list of fake news headlines which they must work with a partner to identify as fake or real.

4. Final Assessment: Exit Slip: name and explain three fake news techniques.

Homework: Go to factcheck.org and take notes on a fake story

Day 2:

1. (Hook/Pre-Assessment)—Discuss cartoon from Junior Scholastic.

2. Small Group Discussion and Analysis of Fake News Sources—Think-Pair-Share.

a. Each student in the group will receive an article which they will individually read and annotate for fake news techniques. These articles were differentiated based on difficulty and content.

b. Students will answer intentionally leveled depth of knowledge discussion questions about which fake news techniques are being used in this article.

c. Students will prepare and share a summary of the story they discussed, as well as one main example of the fake news techniques used.

3. Full class discussion—responsibility of media.

a. Whose responsibility is it to limit or ban fake news? Is censoring fake news limiting American citizens' right to free speech (Facebook CEO Mark Zuckerberg commented on this)? What does the spread of fake news mean for the future of our country? Did we create our own problem by constantly passing around this information?

Homework: Choose one of the discussion questions and respond with a two-paragraph journal entry.

Differentiation Strategies: (Based on Student Profiles)

• A pre-assessment of students' comprehension of the text will be used to determine the intentional group in which each student is placed.

• The lessons were differentiated by process (leveled discussion questions and tasks), product (graphic organizers are different for each group), and content (articles differentiated for each group based on difficulty and the fake news tactics used).

Supplemental Resources:

Before the lesson

1. Pre-assessment.

Day 1:

2. Column from PBS.org for warm-up activity (PDF).
3. Notes on fake news techniques.
4. Fake news indicators handout (see below).
5. Headlines and passages worksheet (see below).
6. Exit Slip question.

Day 2:

7. Cartoon from Junior Scholastics.
8. Depth of knowledge discussion questions inside Think-Pair-Share graphic organizer (Group Activity Directions).
9. Suggested Passages (found in Junior Scholastic article "Fake News Fools Millions!")
   a. "WikiLEAKS confirms Hillary sold weapons to ISIS" from *Political Insider*.
   b. "What surveillance can uncover about you" from *Boston Globe*.
   c. "As Americans Focus on Walking Dead, NATO Troops & US Marines Prep for Russian War on European Soil" from Free Thought Project.
10. Small group discussion rubric to formatively assess students while working.
11. Full class discussion questions.

Fake news indicators handout:

Directions: Use this checklist "look for" indicators of terms used that suggest fake news while reading:

_____ Terminology is used inconsistently by different individuals or organizations in the news media.

_____ Inaccurate examples are provided demonstrating the meaning of the terms.

_____ Emotionally provocative terms or adjectives are used to modify the meaning of terms.

_____ Anecdotes or personal stories are used to demonstrate the meaning of a term or concept, but the anecdote either does not accurately represent the concept or cannot be verified.

_____ Personal or "ad Hominin" attack phrases and terms are used to adversely affect the character and perception of another person or group.

_____ Subtle "dog whistle" phrases and terms are used as a code for a characterization of others or policies and avoid making an overt negative statement about others.

_____ Euphemisms or deceptively pleasant terms are used to create a false and positive image of a potentially negative event or policy.

_____ Slogans or catch phrases are used without complete description as an attempt to convey meaning rather than a full presentation of content.

_____ Labels are given to create a negative perception of persons, groups, or policies.

_____ Term or phrase is often repeated and without further elaboration with the assumption that repetition makes the term or phrase accepted as accurate and increases the chance the term will be more often used and remembered.

Headlines and passages worksheet:

Directions: Determine if the headline and/or the accompanying passage is fake or real news.

Next, discuss with your partner and come to a common conclusion. Finally, explain your reasoning in the space beneath it.

1. "Obama Signs Executive Order Banning the Pledge of Allegiance in Schools Nationwide" from CNN.com.de.

2. "Pope Francis Shocks World, Endorses Donald Trump for President, Releases Statement" from WTOE 5 News.

3. "Survivors of Syrian attack describe chemical bombs falling from sky."

By Angela Dewan, Kareem Khadder, and Holly Yan.

4. Health and Human Services secretary Tom Price says "It's better for our budget if cancer patients die more quickly" from Newslo.

5. "AWFUL: Top Democrats Refuse to Stand, Clap for Navy SEAL Widow Honored by Trump" from The Daily Wire. "Democrats initially stood for the widow. But then they sat. Trump didn't. As his widow wept and mouthed to heaven, 'I love you, baby,' Trump led a round of applause that lasted two minutes. And House minority leader Nancy Pelosi (D-CA) apparently sat there and didn't cheer as the incredible moment progressed, along with Senator Bernie Sanders and others."

ACTIVITY (2) USING PROJECT-BASED LEARNING

Project-based learning provides opportunities for student to apply their knowledge and skills in evaluating the news. A project based upon investigating a real-world news topic can ensure opportunities for student's application of the comprehensive skills and "look for" indicators of real and fake news provided in this book.

The intent of the project based activity is to purposively offer the following educational experiences for students:

Student educational skills and applications:

- Analysis and delineation of a problem,
- Identification and analysis of terms and issues,
- Examination of different perspectives,
- Evaluation of information in the news,
- Determination of appropriate decision made from the news,
- Consideration of potential outcomes and unintended consequences from the decision,
- Student reflection upon the issues,
- Discussion with peers.

The project can be selected either by the instructor or by students from the following list of these or other potential topics:

Potential topics:

Taxes (what kind, how much, who pays),
Regulation (safety, cost, benefit),
Functioning of government (cost, services, private vs. public),
Sex education (comprehensive, abstinence),
Defense (cost, type),
Environment (cost, regulation, type),
Social support programs (costs, type),
Criminal justice (cost, type),
Education (cost, public vs. private, outcomes),
Religious freedom (extent of interference with civil laws),
Weapons and gun control (regulation of use),
Evolution,
Vaccination vs. faked data,
Climate change.

Pedagogical foundations: A constructivist student-centered approach to teaching and learning that provides opportunities for collaborative problem solving. The instructor serves as a facilitator rather than a provider of information. Students are assumed to be engaged in a more active learning mode and gain experience with application of knowledge to practice in real-life dilemmas in their areas of concentration. Projects are considered a best practice that can engage students in higher order thinking.

Structure of tasks to complete:

1. Instructor can assign the project or permit students to select the project topic.
2. Instructor would indicate the:
   • Time constraints;
   • Assignment of students;
   • Roles of students;
   • Forms for students to complete for the project;
   • Scoring standards and rubric for grading student project.
3. The instructor would require the students to complete the following tasks within the project topic:
   a) Issues
   b) Facts
      1. verifiable "look for" real news facts
      2. "look for" facts of fake news

c) Different perspectives or interpretations provided by
   1. real news
   2. fake news

d) Type and sequence of recommendations for action by
   1. real news
   2. fake news

e) Potential positive and negative consequences of the recommended actions by
   1. real news
   2. fake news

Pedagogical techniques to facilitate project discussion:

1. Determine the instructional objective or student skill that the project can clarify, illustrate, or reinforce.
2. Set the agenda—clearly outline the structure noted above and expectations about student behavior and assessment.
3. Probing—asking students for more information or explanation.
4. Follow-up questioning—asking students to identify the consequences of a proposed action.
5. Role-playing—assigning or asking students to assume the perspectives of individuals in the news.
6. Ask for information—asking students to identify overlooked facts or what might be missing in the discussion.
7. Alternative perspective—asking students to identify and discuss the opposite perspective of what was just discussed.
8. Active listening—rephrasing a student response. ("I heard you say.")
9. Redirecting—calling on a student in another part of the room to comment on what was just discussed.
10. Compare and contrast—identify how this project topic situation or solution is the same or different from other projects or examples examined.
11. Positive feedback—reinforce student responses and appropriate use of resources.
12. Summarizing—asking students to identify the major concepts or conclusions learned from the project.

Reflection questions:

1) What information did you feel was most accurate? Why?

_____

_____

2) What information did you feel was the least accurate? Why?

_____

_____

3) Did any of this information make you change your opinion or belief? Why?

_____

_____

ACTIVITY (3) FAKE NEWS BINGO

Have a separate bingo card that contains descriptive words or terms from the issues and checklist "look for" indicators. Students could then seek a real-world example of the terms or indicators to complete the bingo card. Students could work independently or in teams. Students might even listen to a news conference or news program and identify any of the techniques of fake news communication listed in chapter 11 of the book.

Table 14.2 is an example of a fake news bingo card with different "look for" indicators that could be used. Many different combinations of indicators and locations on the bingo cards can provide multiple opportunities for practice:

Table 14.2. Fake news bingo

Fake News

terms to create emotional reaction	"straw man"	small sample size	personal or "ad Hominin" attack	"opt-in" or voluntary participation
urgency	biased sponsor of information	delay an answer	low beginning values in rate of change	restrict access
"leading" questions in surveys or interviews	cherry picking	**fake news free space**	anonymous source	average distorted by a few extremely high or low scores
frame the issue	hypothetical answer	change or redirect the topic	estimated scores used	blame others
counterfactual statement of "what would have happened if"	false equivalence	tables or graphs cut off extremely high or low scores	trial balloon	conspiracy theory

Chapter 15

Recommendations

The only bulwark of continuing liberty is a government strong enough to protect the interests of the people, and a people strong enough and well enough informed to maintain its sovereign control over its government.

—Franklin Delano Roosevelt

The spirit of truth and the spirit of freedom—they are the pillars of society.

—Henrik Ibsen

To form a more perfect union, the Founding Fathers assumed a free press was an unbiased monitor supporting the ability of citizens to make better decisions by warning of inaccurate information and corrupt practices. The warning alarm bells are now ringing and alerting us to the threats to our society from information warfare, with attacks using weapons of false and fake news to influence our choices. We need to avoid becoming refugees seeking a sanctuary from this warfare.

Do we need to form an Evidence Militia of patriots with the "call to bear arms" against the invading Information Barbarians, now at the gates of our society? We cannot let these barbarians enter our society. Do we need to rally around a heroic battle cry? How about: "Remember the Evidence"?

Our democracy can be threatened by fake news and the speed by which the fake news can be disseminated. An informed citizenry can be a protector of the liberty of all in this war.

A society reflects the choices made by its citizens. If a society values truth, then safeguards and protections for truth must be established by each individual and within the educational and societal systems.

INDIVIDUAL RECOMMENDATIONS

In previous chapters, multiple personal biases and the limited knowledge of citizens in evaluating the news were presented. As a citizen, each of us has a personal responsibility to evaluate and distinguish truthful from fake news objectively. Acknowledging and minimizing our personal biases are a necessary first step. The second step is to acquire knowledge to evaluate the news objectively. The final step is the commitment then to make choices based upon objectively verifiable truthful information rather than fake and flimsy news.

Each member of society has a vested interest in others to minimize bias, gain knowledge, and commit to making decisions upon truthful information rather than fake news. If we do not accept this responsibility to others, then we may have guaranteed the "mutually assured self-destruction" of a society just as certainly as if by nuclear war.

Are we able to change our decisions when presented with more accurate, relevant, or sufficient information? Are we able to distinguish real from fake news? Are we able to minimize our biases? These are all questions that each of us needs to answer.

Chapter 13 in this book provides a variety of methods that an individual can apply to distinguish real and fake news. The use of the checklist "look for" indicators in each of the different chapter topics provides a more objective and comprehensive guide for evaluating the news.

This book assists our self-reflection and understanding of how to evaluate news. The hope is that each of us has a commitment to each other—and future generations—to accept the challenge of applying the knowledge of making decisions upon truthful rather than fake news.

EDUCATIONAL POLICY RECOMMENDATIONS

A disturbing observation from a research study is the limited skills and knowledge of students in distinguishing real from fake news (Wineburg, 2016). This lack of knowledge results in "low information" voters who may make decisions upon fake news. The negative effects upon our society are obvious. As noted earlier, President John Adams stated, *"Liberty cannot be preserved with a general knowledge among the people."* What if the people have a limited knowledge in evaluating the news? How does this limited knowledge reduce liberty by making citizens more susceptible to being influenced by fake news?

An educated citizenry is one of the most effective safeguards to our liberties. Increasing calls have been made for improved civic education that combines skills of critical thinking, analysis, and evaluation of evidence in making civic decisions (AAC&U, 2015). These skills may need to be introduced throughout the educational experience of students (Herold, 2016b).

Improved civic knowledge is a needed life skill for each of us. Civic education depends upon several policies and includes: enhanced teacher preparation training (AAC&U, 2017) and development of curricula within the K-12 school grades as proposed in California (Stoltzfus, 2017).

Development of a curriculum with materials and methods of assessing student knowledge of these skills will be an educational policy that is of benefit to all of us. The questions to answer in developing a curriculum are: what type of citizens we want our students to become (Westheimer, 2015), and how to do we provide the necessary educational instruction and information?

The term, CIVILYTICS, is used in this book to indicate the comprehensive necessary preparation and knowledge for citizens in at least three broad skills:

- Media literacy in identifying potential sources of information;
- Data literacy in understanding and analyzing quantitative information;
- Critical thinking skills in evaluating potential evidence and alternative explanations and actions.

Each of these broad skills has additional specific skills. For example, the data literacy may have at least these specific skills such as: understanding tables and graphs; understanding statistics of average, correlation, and standard scores; and understanding the concept of probability.

This expansion of civic education beyond just the call for media literacy is necessary as so much more is involved in distinguishing real from fake news than just checking the sources. A citizen has to be prepared to evaluate all types of information.

The development of this CIVILYTICS knowledge can occur throughout the K-12 and also undergraduate college education. The developmental level of students is important in considering the depth and breadth of instruction. High school and college level students could reasonably be expected to understand and apply the evaluative indicators in this book. Teachers could provide instruction to younger students using a shorter and more basic list of indicators from this book.

Many specific issues will need to be considered in development of an improved civic education. Regardless of the specifics of the curriculum or other educational policies, the need for improved skills is urgent.

Several recommendations are made for improved educational policies and practices:

- *Recommendation 1:* All teacher education preparation programs must include training in the comprehensive civic education skill development included in this book. If teachers are unable to evaluate truth from fake news objectively, then how can we expect teachers to assist students to develop those skills?

- *Recommendation 2:* A civic education examination must be prepared and standards set for all teacher education preparation graduates to pass to receive appropriate state or other professional licensure. This examination provides verification that the prospective teacher has at least appropriate knowledge in distinguishing real from fake news.
- *Recommendation 3:* Specific curricular guides must be prepared, based upon developmental levels of students between middle school and high school. These guides can provide instructional suggestions and resources for this more comprehensive civic education set of skills. Civic education means more than just a general description of how a bill passes into law (or not); so improved civic education requires a more informed citizenry that is capable of differentiating real from fake news.
- *Recommendation 4:* A civic education examination must also be prepared for high school students. This test will provide verification of the knowledge level of students. The test will not be required for graduation as the political controversy would be significant. However, the test results can inform educators of the knowledge and skill level of graduates and any need to modify instruction in any civic education topics where students did not perform as well as expected.

The commitment to improve civic education will require:

- Modification of the curricula;
- Improved training within teacher educator preparation programs;
- Expenditures for necessary educational materials;
- Commitment to assess students and change instructional strategies to improve student understanding.

These recommendations will have costs, but may be minimized with inclusion across traditional courses such as social studies, history, mathematics, and English. The concept of educating students for the common good of society is almost universally accepted, but there is a lack of agreement of which skills to teach students to be good citizens (Westheimer, 2015). The authors of this book believe that students should develop CIVILYTICS skills that include evaluating and distinguishing real and fake news. The cost may not be significant if, as John Stuart Mill stated, "The worth of a state, in the long run, is the worth of the individual composing it."

SOCIETAL POLICY RECOMMENDATIONS

A recurring theme of this book is the need to educate citizens in how objectively to evaluate the news. Unfortunately, pressures within our society are making that a challenging task. These pressures come from court decisions, governmental policies, and political decisions and politicians. Many of these pressures are described within the first hurdle included in chapter 2.

One of the most powerful pressures supporting fake news is the Supreme Court. The first reaction may be of disbelief; but let's objectively look at the evidence. Here are some concerns and recommendations for the courts:

The court has used unverified "facts" presented as Amicus Curiae as a basis for decisions. These "facts" may come from blogs or any source including fake news sources. The justices may then use this information to make decisions that confirm personal bias. The implication is that truth in a Supreme Court may simply reflect the ideology of a justice.

- *Recommendation 5:* Training should be required for justices in data literacy and methodology to obtain necessary knowledge in evaluating research studies and determining accurate real news from fake news.

The court has permitted almost unlimited amounts of money as an anonymous political contribution. Statements of contributors indicate that they expect some influence on policy from their donation to reflect a particular fake news bias or benefit to the exclusion of other contrary, but perhaps, more objectively beneficial policies.

- *Recommendation 6:* Campaign contribution limits must be established to minimize the influence of mega donors potentially to disseminate fake news to a wider audience. The identity of contributors over an established amount ($5,000 might be appropriate) should be a matter of public record to protect the public from potential conflicts of interest and potential influence from fake news sources.

The court has limited the protection from inaccurate or false political ads. The assumption is that the "people" are the only judges of the truth. The implication is that the justices are not the judges of the truth so the "people" may have little protection from fake news.

- *Recommendation 7:* A national campaign review board should be established to review campaign advertising for congressional and presidential elections. Standards for accuracy, relevance, and sufficiency should be established to distinguish real from fake news. Violations of any of those standards should have a consequence of a financial penalty or suspension of campaign activities. Society needs to have protection from fake political news when making decisions about political candidates.

• *Recommendation 8:* The courts must also be open to further examining the issue of fake news in the context of additional concepts such as "obstruction of justice" and/or potential harm. Could not fake news obstruct obtaining an accurate or just decision and also contribute to potential harm? Free and unbridled speech that permits fake news needs to have more legal protections and effective consequences because of potential harm.

Governmental policies have also contributed to the growth of inaccurate or fake news. For example, The Fairness Doctrine was eliminated by the Federal Communications Commission in 1987. Radio and television airwaves are considered a public resource; but more groups and individuals wanted to purchase airwaves than were available. Therefore, the doctrine required a "balanced" presentation of controversial issues as a right of the public to be better informed.

The result of eliminating this doctrine is the growth of more focused and "unbalanced" rather than "balanced" content in cable television, talk radio, and other media. A single view or belief is presented almost as if propaganda without concern for accuracy. Contrary information is ignored or disparaged. The irony is that presenting just a single view contributes to greater susceptibility as citizens may "trust" and be less critical of news from that source.

• *Recommendation 9:* Reestablish the Fairness Doctrine to provide multiple perspectives and evidence regarding controversial issues. Multiple perspectives and contrary evidence permit citizens to be better informed in evaluating the news.

Political processes and politicians also contribute to the proliferation of fake news and to a single view in these ways:

Gerrymandering is a process by which congressional districts are drawn and configured in a manner by which boundaries may have vastly irregular shapes in order to concentrate voters of one political party in one district or to minimize the influence of voters of a political party in a district. The result is congressional districts where the incentive of representatives is to play to the narrow confirmation bias of the views or opinions of the constituency even if the views are from fake news. The representative is not forced to defend views to a wider audience or contrary information when evaluating the truth of the news.

- *Recommendation 10:* Congressional districts need to be drawn to minimize the concentration of voters with a particular view. Democracy thrives when presentation and debate of competing views are presented with the goals of understanding and consensus. Drawing congressional districts either upon a geographical basis with no extreme distortions in the dimensions or by an independent commission may be appropriate to minimize the potential distortions from a narrow constituency.

Politicians have also attempted to restrict access of some media journalists or to use only select media journalists. The attempt is to control the news by preventing a free press from asking questions to challenge the truth of information or to detect fake news. Media journalists who report what the politician wants are often rewarded with "exclusive" information or interviews.

This practice of restricted access is of particular concern as our Founding Fathers assumed that the role of a free press is to protect the public by obtaining accurate information and informing the public of deceptions. Control of the media is often one of the first steps in governments that may even attempt to distribute fake news as the truth.

- *Recommendation 11:* Media journalists should adopt a professional practice policy that all press conferences, significant events, addresses, or access to government officials are open to all accredited media. Restricted access should be opposed by all media, and they should not permit "exclusive" coverage by any. A "sunshine" policy should be adopted to permit a transparent and open access and questioning of government officials. Remember, the government officials work for the public and the public pays their salary.

Journalists also contribute to the growth of fake news by not having sufficient training for analysis of information. How can a journalist determine the accuracy, relevance, or sufficiency of information if he or she does not have the knowledge of media literacy, data literacy, and critical thinking skills? The pressures of being first with a news item create little time for careful analysis.

- *Recommendation 12:* Journalists should have required training in methods of data analysis and critical thinking skills as components of professional training. Media journalists should also include analysis and objectively verifiable interpretations of news events to assist the citizen in distinguishing accurate and fake news. The rush to meet a deadline needs to be reexamined as this rush creates a potential problem of lack of time to verify and distinguish real and fake news. Speed kills on the highway of reporting accurate news.

Another contributor to fake news is simply the behavior of the leaders of our government and leaders in society. Some of our leaders accept and even create fake news and conspiracy theories while denying contrary factual information. What does this say about our society if our leaders model these inappropriate behaviors?

- *Recommendation 13:* Leaders of our society need to lead by example in objectively pursuing truthful information and rejecting fake news. We are judged by our actions and these actions speak more loudly than any words. Sadly, this recommendation may be the most challenging to accomplish.

Importance of fake news issue:
Our society also faces international challenges from cyberattacks and dissemination of fake news and propaganda. The purposes of these attacks may be financial. However, even more importantly, these attacks may be an attempt to destabilize our very government and society.

Creating doubts, distorting information, using blatant lies, and having fake news are weapons as powerful as any military armaments in destroying our life and society. Being warned of the danger from these attacks means that each of us must be prepared and armed as citizens in the war against fake news.

Discussion questions:

(1) Ask students to identify any actions needed to protect us from the harmful effects of fake news.
(2) Ask students how they can develop news literacy and respond to the challenges of objectively evaluating news in making civic decisions.

FINAL THOUGHT:

H. G. Wells observed, "Human history becomes more and more a race between education and catastrophe." The hope is that this book provides assistance preparing each of us to defend our society.
                           —We will win this war!—

References

Anderson, Chris. (2017). Does Steve Bannon live in Sarasota County? Because he is registered to vote. *The Sarasota Herald-Tribune*, January 24, 2017.

Association of American Colleges & Universities (AAC&U). (2015). *Civic Learning and Democratic Engagement: A Crucible Moment*. Washington, D.C.: AACU.

Association of American Colleges & Universities (AAC&U). (2017). Perspectives—educators wage war against fake news. *AAC&U News*, January, February 2017.

Barbour, C. & Streb, M., eds. (2011). *Clued in to Politics*. Los Angeles: Sage.

Berliner, D. & Glass, G. (2014). *50 Myths and Lies That Threaten America's Public Schools*. New York: Teachers College Press.

Best evidence encyclopedia. (2014). *Standards for Research-Proven Programs*. Johns Hopkins University. Retrieved from April 26, 2017 www.thebee@bestevidence.org.

Biesecker, M. & Borenstein, S. (2017). *EPA Science Under Scrutiny by Trump Political Staff*. Associated Press, January 25, 2017.

Blastland, M. & Dilnot, A. (2009). *The Numbers Game*. New York: Gotham Books.

Blinder, A. (2017). Kansas lawmakers uphold governor's veto of tax increase. *The New York Times*, February 22, 2017.

Burns, C. (2008). *Deadly Decisions*. Amherst, New York: Prometheus Books.

Chabris, C. & Simons, D. (2010). *The Invisible Gorilla.* New York: Crown Publishers.

Cialdini, R. (2009). *Influence: Science and Practice*. Boston: Pearson Education.

Cialdini, R. (2016). *Pre-suasion: A Revolutionary Way to Influence and Persuade*. New York: Simon & Schuster.

Council for Exceptional Children. (2014). Council for exceptional children standards for evidence-based practices in special education. Council for Exceptional Children, Arlington, Virginia.

Crews Jr., C. (2017). *The Ten Thousand Commandments* (2016 edition). Washington, D.C.: Competitive Enterprise Institute.

Crocco, M., Halvorsen, A, Jacobsen, R., & Segall, A. (2017). Teaching with Evidence. *Kappan*, vol. 98 (7), pp. 67–71.

Danilova, M. (2017). *DeVos to Face Questions Over Schools, Conservative Activism.* Associated Press, January 16, 2017.

D'Antonio, M. (2017). Lying worked for Donald Trump—so why stop now? *CNN,* January 24, 2017.

Davidson, A. (2017). What Trump wants Bill O'Reilly, and all of us, to forget. *The New Yorker,* February 6, 2017.

D'Orio, W. (2017). Avoiding the fake news trap. *Education Update,* vol. 59 (4), pp. 1, 4–5.

Eckhouse, L. (2017). When numbers lie. *The Washington Post,* February 14, 2017.

Erickson, A. (2017). Trump called the news media an "enemy of the American People." *The Washington Post,* February 18, 2017.

Gawande, A. (2009). *The Checklist Manifesto.* New York: Metropolitan Books, Henry Holt and Company, LLC.

Gertz, B. (2017). *iWar: War and Peace in the Information Age.* New York: Threshold Editions, an imprint of Simon & Schuster, Inc.

Goldstein, N., Martin, S., & Cialdini, R. (2008). *Yes! 50 Scientifically Proven Ways to Be Persuasive.* New York: Simon & Schuster.

Gomez, H. J. (2016). Meet the Ohio politicians who prepared us for Donald Trump. *The Plain Dealer,* October 25, 2016.

Green, G. & Coder, J. (2017). *Household Income Trends.* Sentier Research, LLC., Annapolis, Maryland, January, 2017.

Herold, B. (2016a). "Fake news," bogus tweets raise stakes for media literacy. *Education Week,* vol. 36 (14), December 8, 2016.

Herold, B. (2016b). Media literacy vs. bogus news. *Education Week,* vol. 36 (15), December 14, 2016.

Hotez, P. (2017). How the anti-vaxxers are winning. *The New York Times,* February 8, 2017.

Janke, R. W. & Cooper, B. S. (2014). *Errors in Evidence-Based Decision Making: Improving and Applying Research Literacy.* Lanham, MD: Rowman & Littlefield.

Joint Committee of the American Educational Research Association, American Psychological Association, and National Council on Measurement in Education. (2014). *Standards for educational and psychological testing.* American Educational Research Association, Washington, D.C.

Kaczynsk, A. & Massie, C. (2017). Trump cabinet nominee Steven Mnuchin is also registered to vote in two states. *CNN Politics,* January 25, 2017.

Kahneman, D. (2011). *Thinking Fast and Slow.* New York: Farrar, Strauss & Giroux.

Kaplan, J. (ed.). (2002) *Bartlett's Familiar Quotations (17th edition).* New York: Little, Brown & Company.

Kolbert, E. (2017). Why facts don't change over minds. *The New Yorker,* February 27, 2017.

Lehrer, J. (2009). *How We Decide.* New York: Houghton Mifflin Harcourt Publishing Company.

Leibovich, M. (2004). George Tenet's "slam-dunk" into the history books. *The Washington Post,* June 4, 2004.

Levitt, J. (2007). *The Truth About Voter Fraud.* New York: The Brennan Center for Justice.

Liptak, A. (2014). Seeking facts, justices settle for what briefs tell them. *The New York Times*, September 2, 2014.

Lopez, G. (2017). Trump: The murder rate is at a 45 year high, actual statistics: That's not factually true. *CNBC Online*, February 8, 2017.

Mande, J. (2016). Follow the money. *The New Yorker*, November 28, 2016.

Massie, C. (2017). WH official: we'll say "fake news" until media realizes attitude of attacking the president is wrong. *CNN Politics*, February 7, 2017.

McGinty, J. (2016). Why the government puts a dollar value on life. *The Wall Street Journal*, March 25, 2016.

Miller, G. & Entous, A. (2017). President tried to counter stories on Russia, officials say. *The Washington Post*, February 25, 2017.

Moore, M. (2016). Trump Winery is trying to hire foreign workers. *The New York Post,* December 22, 2016.

Newberg, A. & Waldman, M. (2006). *Why We Believe What We Believe*. New York: Free Press.

Office of the Director of National Intelligence. (2017). *Assessing Russian Activities and Intention in Recent U.S. Elections: The Analytic Process and Cyber Incident Attribution*. Washington, D.C.: ODNI.

Ornstein, N. & Abramowitz, A. (2016). Stop the polling insanity. *The New York Times*, May 20, 2016.

Paul, R. & Elder, L. (2007). *Educational Fads*. California: The Foundation for Critical Thinking, Dillon Beach.

Phillip, A. & DeBonis, M. (2017). Without evidence, Trump tells lawmakers of 3 million to 5 million "illegal" ballots cost him the popular vote. *The Washington Post*, January 24, 2017.

The Plain Dealer. (2017). *Tax cuts won't help Ohio get stronger*. February 10, 2017. p. E2.

Ravitch, D. (2013). *Reign of Error*. New York: Knopf.

Reardon, S., Kalogrides, D., & Shores, K. (2017). The geography of racial/ethnic test scores gaps (CEPA Working Paper No.16–10). Retrieved from April 26, 2017 Stanford Center for Education Policy Analysis: http://cepa.stanford.edu/wp16-10.

Roth, Z. (2015). Congressman uses misleading graph to smear Planned Parenthood. *MSNBC*, September 29, 2015.

Schipani, V. (2017). Rise in autism cases inflated. *The Plain Dealer*, February 26, 2017.

Shane, S. (2017). From headline to photograph, a fake news masterpiece. *The New York Times*, January 18, 2017.

Shermer, M. (2011). *The Believing Brain*. New York: Times Books, Henry Holt and Company LLC.

Specter, M. (2017). Trump's dangerous support for conspiracies about autism and vaccines. *The New Yorker*, January 11, 2017.

Stolberg, S. (2012). Gingrich stuck to caustic path in ethics battles. *The New York Times*, January 26, 2012.

Stoltzfus, K. (2017). California mulls curriculum to teach about "fake news." *Education Week*, vol. 36, 19, January 25, 2017.

Superville, D. & Lemire, J. (2017). Trump promotes school choice in Florida visit. *The Philadelphia Tribune,* March 4, 2017.

Tani, M. (2017). As an expert witness for Whole Foods, Kellyanne Conway gave testimony that was deemed "fundamentally flawed" and thrown out. *Business Insider,* March 14, 2017.

Thaler, R. & Sunstein, C. (2009). *Nudge.* New York: Penguin Books.

U.S. Department of Education. (1983). *A nation at risk: an imperative for educational reform.* Washington, D.C.

U.S. Department of Education. (2012). *Advancing Civic Learning and Engagement in Democracy: A Road Map and Call to Action.* Washington, D.C.: USDE.

U.S. Department of Education, Institute of Education Sciences (IES), What Works Clearinghouse. (2016, September). *What Works Clearinghouse Procedures and Standards Handbook (version 3.0).* Retrieved from http://whatworks.ed.gov.

Valenza, J. (2016). Truth, truthiness, triangulation: A news toolkit for post-truth world. *School Library Journal,* November 26, 2016.

Weber, P. (2016). Grand jury indicts leader behind Planned Parenthood videos. *The San Diego Union-Tribune,* January 25, 2016.

Weir, K. (2017). Why we believe alternative facts. *Monitor on Psychology,* vol. 48 (5), pp. 34–39.

Westheimer, J. (2015). *What Kind of Citizen?* New York: Teachers College Press.

White, E. (2017). *Early and Often? 31 People Voted Twice in Michigan Election.* Detroit, MI: Associated Press, February 9, 2017.

Wiggins, G. & McTighe, J. (2005). *Understanding by design (2nd edition).* Alexandria: Association for Supervision and Curriculum Development.

Willingham, A. J. (2016). Here's how to outsmart fake news in your Facebook. CNN feed. (CNN, 2016, http://www.cnn.com/2016/11/18/tech/how-to-spot-fake-misleading-news- trnd/).

Wineburg, S. (lead author). (2016). *Evaluating Evidence: The Cornerstone of Civic Online Reasoning (Executive Summary).* Stanford History Education Group, Palo Alto, California, November 22, 2016.

Zedeck, S. (editor in chief). (2014). *APA Dictionary of Statistics and Research Methods.* Washington, D.C: American Psychological Association.

Index

Note: page numbers in italics indicate figures.

About the Authors

Robert W. Janke taught high school classes in history and social studies; conducted individual diagnostic assessments of over 3,000 students as a school psychologist and licensed psychologist; and is a professor in teacher education at Baldwin Wallace University. His interest in accuracy of news developed from his early experience as a teenage copyboy and writer for the community page of a daily newspaper. He received a Ph. D. from the University of Michigan in the Combined Program in Education and Psychology. His professional educational interests are in the areas of research and assessment methods.

Bruce S. Cooper, Ph.D., is Professor Emeritus, of Education Administration and Public Policy, Graduate School of Education, Fordham University, New York, New York from 1981 to 2016. He also taught at University of Pennsylvania, University of London, and Dartmouth College, after receiving his doctorate at the University of Chicago with Donald A. Erickson, as his mentor. Cooper has written 45 books on education politics and policy, including The Handbook of Education Politics and Policy, in two editions with Lance D. Fusarelli and James Cibulka. He served as President of the Politics of Education Association (PEA) in 1983 and a founding member of Associates for Research on Private Education (ARPE). He received the Jay D. Scribner Award for Mentoring from the University Council for Education Administration (UCEA).

CPSIA information can be obtained
at www.ICGtesting.com
Printed in the USA
BVOW03*0837111017
496769BV00011B/7/P